Mrs Fry's Diary

About the author:

Edna is the devoted wife of Stephen Fry and the mother of his various children.

Mrs Fry's Diary

Mrs Stephen Fry

First published in Great Britain in 2010 by Hodder & Stoughton
An Hachette UK company

1

A CIP catalogue record for this title is available from the British Library

ISBN 978 1444 72077 8

Typeset in Century Old Style by Hewer Text UK Ltd, Edinburgh

Printed and bound by Clays Ltd, St Ives plc

Hodder & Stoughton policy is to use papers that are natural, renewable and recyclable products and made from wood grown in sustainable forests. The logging and manufacturing processes are expected to conform to the environmental regulations of the country of origin.

Hodder & Stoughton Ltd
338 Euston Road
London NW1 3BH

www.hodder.co.uk

For Stephen and the bills.

Foreword

It's always pleased me that my wife has had a hobby. I thought it was stitch-work she was doing. I had no idea she had written a book. That she did so using needle and thread rather than keyboard and computer, just to keep up the pretence, shows her commitment and force of character. I can't pretend I'm pleased, but nor can I deny that I am proud. Damned proud. If she makes a habit of it or starts to embark on whistlestop publicity tours, I fear for the household and the children's meals. But yes, I am proud. How much I enjoy or bemoan seeing my life delineated in such pitiless detail I shall leave you all to guess. But proud, yes, I am proud of the little woman. Bless her.

Stephen Fry

January

1 Saturday

Every January 1st is exactly the same – a cold grey afternoon, nothing on the telly and Stephen with his head down the toilet, belching the theme to *Dr Zhivago*. Must be Groundhogmanay. Apparently he spent the night unconscious in the S & M club car park. This morning I had to pay £50 to have his nipples unclamped.

Made our New Year's resolutions. Mine is to be even more patient and understanding than I already am and Stephen's is to give up swearing. And kebabs. And karaoke. And tequila. And her at number 38. Now all I have to do is get him to sign it while he's still only semi-conscious. Thank goodness for Citizens

Advice. Who knew there was such a thing as a post-nup?

2 Sunday

Felching & Sons' sale started today. Managed to get a few post-Christmas presents. A Tickle-Me-Kylie for Stephen Junior and a Nintendo Puu for little Brangelina – apparently it's like a Wii, only you play it sitting down.

3 Monday

At last, the children are back at school. Or amusement arcade. Or wherever it is they go from Monday to Friday. And her at number 38's husband's away again, so Stephen's shot out on his window-cleaning round.

Enjoyed a nice cuppa this morning with a HobNob and Jeremy Kyle. There was a woman on there who'd been married 16 years without realising her husband was gay. Extraordinary! Which reminds me, it's our 16th anniversary in a few weeks. What a coincidence. Personally, I think the key to a successful marriage is maintaining separate interests. I have my cooking, my pottery and my love of 19th-century literature and Stephen has his *Razzle* magazines.

4 Tuesday

Coffee this morning with Mrs Norton and Mrs Winton in the Cuppa Cabana. They do an excellent special Colombian blend – apparently the owner imports it herself from Bogotá. She gets a fresh delivery every week by courier. I have to say it's a little too pungent for my tastes, although it certainly gives you a buzz. I prefer to go for the decaf, which, oddly, has the same effect.

Popped into Foodland afterwards to pick up a few things. It really is the little woman's paradise, just like they say on the commercials. They boast the lowest prices in the area and the widest range of artificial additives and chemicals of any supermarket chain. It certainly helps when you're trying to stretch your meagre housekeeping, plus I have to get our food there anyway, as Stephen's Waitrose intolerant.

SHOPPING LIST:

Spam – multipack
Cup-a-Fruit
I Can't Believe It's Not Lager
It Ain't Necessarily Soap
Bedroom ceiling mirror polish

5 Wednesday

Twelfth Night. We took the Christmas decorations down today. I say we – I took the decorations down. If I waited for Stephen to do it, the house would still be looking like an elves' lap-dancing club in July. It took him three years just to put that bookshelf up. It'll probably be another three before he buys a book.

6 Thursday

Goodness, what a day for a power cut! Stephen and I were freezing this morning. Our bedroom was like an ice box. Fortunately, the kids were fine. We never switch on the heater in their bedroom anyway, otherwise they won't feel the benefit when they go outside. It was so cold, Stephen had no choice but to go to work and I was forced to spend the afternoon with Mrs Winton in her maisonette. She told me all about this new Reiki fortune teller she's just started seeing. First she gives you an intense scalp massage, then she reads your dandruff. I'd love to have my scalp massaged some time, but apparently they can't do it without removing your hat.

7 Friday

Topless Tequila Karaoke at Sombrero's tonight. I never go with Stephen. I always get so nervous when he performs. Besides, it's impossible to get babysitters, especially since the ASBOs. It's the regional quarter finals tonight. No doubt, if Stephen nails Lady Gaga on the mechanical bull, I'll have a semi to deal with . . .

Past midnight now. No sign of Stephen. Knowing him, he'll have gone on to a club to celebrate or drown his sorrows. I do hope he doesn't come back in one of his kinky moods again. Last week he insisted we try a bit of bondage. Can't say it did anything for me. I bruised my knee on the sideboard and he ended up in Halfords. Perhaps next time only one of us should wear a blindfold.

8 Saturday

Oh dear. Stephen smeared his you-know-what with superglue again last night. I'd love to tell someone about it but my lips are sealed.

9 Sunday

Typical Sunday morning. Stephen was in his Rudolph Valentino mood this week – he insisted I join him in his 'tent of love'. Of course, it was just a bed sheet before he got excited. I do wish he'd give up this roleplay malarkey. If it's not doctor and receptionist, it's gladiator and slave girl or aerobics instructor and regional head of town planning. The other week he wanted us to play amusement arcade manager and naughty schoolgirl. Well, I thought. In for a penny . . .

Managed to persuade Stephen to drive me to Ikea in the afternoon – I told him it was the new

Apple gadget. Unfortunately, he had one of his panic attacks in the store. I'd forgotten all about his claustrophobia. And fear of anything Swedish. It all stems, apparently, from the time he was stuck in a lift with ABBA.

In the end, it took two puffs on his inhaler and half my Valium to calm him down. Thank goodness we didn't go in my sister's Volvo. Still, it gave me time to get the tea cosy I was looking for (or, as they call it, SchlurpWully) and I found a lovely new bedside lamp (LiteFondl). Ironically, next to the futon Stephen fell asleep on (NobEd).

10 Monday

We told Stephen Junior that he's adopted this evening. He isn't, but there was nothing on TV.

11 Tuesday

Read an article about how some frustrated women use cooking to compensate for the lack of . . . well . . . marital shenanigans. How ridiculous!

Cooking one of my favourite dishes today. Here's the recipe:

Spam Rumpy Pumpy

A robust, filling and intensely satisfying dish. Serves one.

Ingredients:
1 family-sized tin Spam, opened
Extra slutty olive oil
500 ml whipping cream
Zest of 2 Jif lemons
Allspice

Pre-rolled sponge
2 dozen oysters
1.5 litres Blue Nun

1. Preset washing machine to mark 8.
2. Carefully ease meat out of can and lay on flat surface. Season, rolling and teasing gently until lightly flustered.
3. When you have the required length, braise tenderly, slowly raising the heat until sufficient hardening occurs and the juices begin to flow. Firmly rub in oil to maintain optimum moistness.
4. Fill your bowl with cream and whip into frenzy, adding a little zest. Smear over meat and sponge gently.
5. Fold and toss vigorously until completely engorged. Leave to bubble away. Drink Blue Nun, eat oysters and lean against washing machine until thoroughly drizzled.
6. Serve with broccoli, new potatoes and a cigarette.

12 Wednesday

Went to the cinema this evening. It was a choice between a Woody Allen film and *Avatar*, but I can't stand those ridiculous glasses, so we watched *Avatar*.

13 Thursday

Brangelina's so cute. Apparently at school today she had a playground wedding. Her best friend LaToya was the head bridesmaid, her little classmate Shane played the groom (looking a little worse for wear after yesterday's playground stag night), the deputy head Miss Morgan officiated and the school solicitor drew up the pre-nup. They even had a professional photographer. I say professional, more an enthusiastic amateur. Long Range Len did a lovely job if you ignore the railings and his net curtain. It's so nice to see children using their imaginations. Next week they're having a playground divorce.

14 Friday

Just discovered a packet of little blue pills in Stephen's pocket. I've told him to think long and hard before taking them.

15 Saturday

The twins' birthday today. Sadly, we were too late to book a party at Build-A-Bear so we went to Do-A-Doll instead. Asbo and Subo had a lovely time. The place was festooned with balloons – all the colours of the rainbow and ribbed for our pleasure. The staff did a tremendous job, leading enthusiastic renditions of 'Happy Birthday', 'The Wheels on the Bus' and 'Eskimo Nell'. They'd arranged party games – Pass the Parcel and Pin the Tail on Donkey Dave – and Booboo the clown was a big hit with his highly creative and anatomically precise balloon animals.

After the party food, the children all got to inflate their own doll and they could even choose the colour of its ultra-realistic hair. The two hours flew by – Stephen particularly enjoyed Sally the Stripping Squirrel – and everyone went home happy with a party bag filled with all sorts of weird and wonderful toys. A great success!

16 Sunday

A nice, relaxing day. I must remember to thank Mrs Winton for putting me on to that feng shui. I have to say it really works! I feel so much calmer since we moved the children's beds into the garage.

17 Monday

Had a lovely lunch with Mrs Norton at the new vegetarian restaurant on the high street,

Debbie Does Salad. Very peculiar, though. She said she'd been watching television the other night and seen someone who looked the spitting image of my Stephen. And he wasn't on *Crimewatch* or *Police, Benefit Cheats, Action.* Some intellectual quiz programme called *Mock Your IQ* or something. Apparently this chap's the host. Must remember to Sky Plus it.

Decided to take a break from the kitchen and have a takeaway tonight. No luck. Tried to order a Domino's pizza but they had no delivery boys available. Apparently one of them had an accident. He fell over, knocking another one over, who knocked another one over . . .

18 Tuesday

Stephen Junior's Parents' Evening today. It was so lovely to finally meet his teacher, Ms Woolley, after her extended leave. I must say she's looking a lot better now. She finally seems to have that twitch under control. She seemed terribly pleased with Stephen Junior's progress this year, or at least the two weeks she's spent with him. She did say he was struggling a bit with his English, but then he gets that from his father. And he's also struggling with his Maths. And his Geography. And his History. And his Science. But he looks set for a grade C in Metalwork and Domestic Violence and apparently, he's already got an ADHD so I was terribly proud. The meeting went swimmingly – unlike his swimming – until Ms Woolley suggested that his results and general demeanour might benefit from a better diet. I'm afraid the rest of the evening is a bit of a blur.

19 Wednesday

Saw Ms Woolley again. I must say the ward looked delightful – lovely wallpaper. I don't know what came over me. Took her a batch of my special lemon ketchup brownies to cheer her up.

20 Thursday

Had to buy another box of Kleenex for Hugh Junior today. I blame myself. Last time I cleared up his bedroom floor, I accidentally dropped 50 pence. Now he thinks there's a sperm fairy. It's costing me a fortune.

21 Friday

I've been telling Stephen for months to get his glasses fixed. If it wasn't for his homing instinct he'd never even make it to the Red Lion's Karaoke Night, although he still managed to win, somehow. Apparently the audience loved his renditions of 'I've Got You Under My Sink' and 'Some Whore Over the Rainbow'.

22 Saturday

What an exciting day! After months of waiting, the new shopping mall – the Shangri-la Centre – finally opened this morning. It's in the industrial estate just off the ring road. It took a while to find it because the sat nav in the Transit's broken (Stephen tried to feed it curry sauce last week on the way back from the dog track). If it hadn't been for Stephen Junior's ankle tracking bracelet we'd never have found it. I must say, though, it was definitely worth the three-and-a-half-hour journey. It was a spectacular affair. They had a ventriloquist and a meat raffle. All the local papers were there and the centre was officially opened by Cristal Braithwaite from series seven of *Big Brother*, who cut a giant credit card in two. Sadly, Stephen had to stay in the car park until she had finished, due to the restraining order. Oddly, one passer-by asked me why Stephen hadn't been asked to open it himself. Silly man. As if anyone would want a window cleaner to open a shopping mall! He has enough trouble opening his own front door most nights.

After the grand opening, we wandered around the centre. It was breathtaking – all gleaming and white, like a giant A & E department. And there was barely any graffiti or vomit. They had every shop you could want, all under one roof. If it had a roof – apparently, that's due to be finished in April.

We skipped excitedly in and out of Primark, 90pWorld and Tattoos 'R' Us before finally heading over to the food court. And what an array greeted us there! All the major fast-food chains – The Toast Factory, Yo! Mince and Sandwich! Sandwich! Sandwich! In the end, we settled on a Bucket o' Cheddar from Cheese Louise. Of course, it couldn't compare with my culinary masterpieces, but it definitely hit the spot.

I have to say it was a truly magical day out. We so rarely get the chance to do something like that as a family, what with Stephen being banned from the bowling alley, the municipal swimming pool and France.

23 Sunday

How annoying. Was about to watch that *IQ* programme Mrs Norton was going on about, when Stephen's foot accidentally slipped through the television screen. That's the third time this month. Thank goodness his mate, Reasonably Honest Al, seems to have an endless supply of the things.

24 Monday

Record takings for Stephen on his window-cleaning round today. Passers-by kept throwing money into his bucket – they thought he was a living statue. Honestly, that man's so lazy. He even gets his *Razzle* magazine on audiobook. He particularly enjoys the Listeners' Wives section.

My mother rang this evening. She's off to Fuengirola with her pool cleaner next week and she wanted my advice about bikini waxing.

She's thinking of having a Brazilian, but I think at her age it can be a bit of a grey area.

25 Tuesday

Had a phone call from Mrs Norton this morning. She said she was busy on her computer the other night – cancelling more of Graham's Lithuanian brides – and she found something called Twitter. She says Stephen's on it. A lot, apparently. And all this time I thought he was just gambling away our holiday savings on Texas Hold 'Em. Some kind of social network thingummybob, she says. I'd better check out his laptop. Goodness only knows what a barely literate window cleaner has to write about.

Oh my giddy aunt! I've just looked at what Stephen's been writing on this Twitter thing. Opera this, concertos that. That man and his imagination! I don't know where he gets it all. According to him, the other night he was at the

Royal Albert Hall enjoying a scintillating interpretation of *Der Ring des Nibelungen*'s *Götterdämmerung*, when I know for a fact he was down the King's Head. He never misses Half-price Bacardi Breezer and Pork Scratchings Night. I must say, all this is very troubling. It's almost as if I don't know the real him at all. Perhaps we should be doing more things together. Things that don't involve banana flavoured lubrication.

26 Wednesday

Time to do the washing. Just realised Stephen's still wearing his December pants. Spam Bourguignon for dinner.

27 Thursday

Incredibly, I managed to persuade Stephen to come with me to the local community college open night tonight. I've decided to enrol on

Creative Writing for the Middle-Aged Housewife, while Stephen's plumped for Intermediate Spinster Spanking.

28 Friday

What terrible luck! Hugh Junior fell on the icy school playground this morning and twisted his ankle. We were hoping for at least a broken leg. It's not as if I didn't push him hard enough. Last year we got a fortnight in Benidorm out of Brangelina's fractured wrist, thanks to So-U-Claim.

29 Saturday

The snow's falling heavier this evening. Stephen just texted to say he might be stuck in the pub all night. He hasn't even left the house yet.

30 Sunday

Our 16th wedding anniversary. Who would have thought? Apparently, 16 is Tupperware. According to Stephen, at any rate. I feel so silly now, buying him that diamond-encrusted gold signet ring and chain set. Still, he didn't seem to object. Luckily, Stephen's karaoke injury compensation came through just in time, so we're off to a show and a slap-up meal tonight. I can't wait. I can't remember when we last went out together, just the two of us. The last time must have been our honeymoon. Of course, strictly speaking, that wasn't just the two of us. Although it was nice of the bouncers to let us take the pram into the casino.

Amazingly, we've found someone to take care of all our kids tonight. Social Services won't normally take more than two at a time. Stephen's dressed up to the nines in his best Hawaiian shirt and leather trousers and I've had my hat specially reupholstered for the occasion. I'll tell you all about it, Dear Diary, when we get back . . .

Goodness, what a night! What a show! Such timing. Such precision. Such incredible grace. I have to say, when it comes to thoroughly spectacular cultural entertainment, it doesn't get any better than Monster Trucks on Ice. Such a shame Stephen got over-excited and the manager of the arena had to ask him to leave. Of course, Stephen being Stephen, he wouldn't go quietly. He swore, he emptied his bucket of buffalo wings over row J and finally gave the manager the finger. His giant foam one.

Still, he calmed down once we got to the restaurant. After his first four lagers, anyway. Mrs Biggins recommended it to me. She and her Chris have been to the Rings of Fire curry house several times. It's a fantasy-theme restaurant where all the waiters dress up in costumes. The smaller ones are hobbits and the rest are wizards and orcs. We had a hobbit, although I must say there was no discernible difference in the quality of service. All in all, it was a thoroughly enjoyable experience. We had a wonderful time. In the end, Stephen and I went for the C.S. Lewis Special set meal. It's like the regular set meal, only naanier.

31 Monday

Just time for a quick entry while Stephen gargles and scratches himself in the bathroom. You know, I'm glad I decided to write this diary. In all the hustle and bustle of day to day life, it's so easy to forget how lucky you really are. This evening, for example. Me washing the pots and doing the ironing, Stephen lying on the sofa with a can of lager in one hand and his genitals in the other, watching *Dame Kiri Te Kanawa Does the Funniest Things*, and the children all safely tucked up in bed looking at their internet porn. I really am blessed.

February

1 Tuesday

Oh dear. Poor Brangelina's still having nightmares. They began a few weeks ago after her teacher mysteriously spontaneously combusted. She was really quite traumatised, particularly as she was the only child in the classroom at the time. It didn't help when the head teacher confiscated her lighter. If ever she needed a smoke it was then, poor thing. Stephen started to read her bedtime stories to see if that helped, but if anything it only made things worse. I spoke to Mrs Winton about it when I popped round for a herbal coffee and she told me we should hang a dreamcatcher over her bed. I'd never heard of such a thing, but apparently they catch all your bad dreams and allow you to have a restful night's sleep.

I expected Stephen to pooh-pooh the idea but he was surprisingly enthusiastic and even made one himself – out of one of my hanging baskets and a badger he ran over last week in the van. Brangelina looked a little sceptical – or possibly terrified, it's so hard to tell with children – but I'm sure she'll get used to it.

2 Wednesday

Social Services called round this morning but I refused to let them in. Last time, they wanted to give us our kids back.

3 Thursday

Disappointed that my first creative writing class was cancelled due to the weather, although the evening wasn't a complete write-off. All that gorgeous, newly fallen snow did bring out our romantic side, so we went out to make snow angels. We managed to knock over 12 snowmen before Stephen crashed the van.

4 Friday

Went to the garden centre this afternoon. We didn't buy anything. We just like to pretend we've got a garden.

5 Saturday

An early start this morning. Stephen and I popped along to the recreation ground to watch Hugh Junior in his first game for the school under-thirteens, the Midwich Cuckoos. It was all very exciting. I don't know much about football but he seemed to play terribly well. So well, in fact, that the umpire said he could go and have a rest after only 10 minutes! Stephen was glowing with fatherly pride, particularly when Hugh Junior was given the red Man of the Match card. All in all, it was terrific fun. We even joined in the Glasgow Wave, which is like a Mexican Wave crossed with a tsunami.

6 Sunday

Woke this morning to the sound of church bells. I'd better tell the kids to take them back before the vicar notices.

7 Monday

Beginning to wonder whether Stephen still finds me as attractive as he used to. I caught him watching me in the bath earlier and I'm sure he was mentally dressing me. Maybe we need some time to ourselves, away from the kids, to rekindle the flame – somewhere romantic, like Rome or Paris. Perhaps if I leave a few brochures lying around he'll get the hint. Or I could roll them up and hit him around the head with them . . .

8 Tuesday

Very disappointing. Creative writing class was cancelled again, due to it being a dark and stormy night.

9 Wednesday

I have to say, Stephen's home-made dreamcatcher has proved a great success. Brangelina hasn't had a single nightmare for a week. And hopefully that will continue when she's finally prepared to go back into her bedroom.

10 Thursday

What an extraordinary day. No sooner had I woken up than Stephen had blindfolded me and bundled me into his van. Normally, it's at least lunchtime before we do anything like that.

I was beginning to get slightly concerned until he kissed me gently on the cheek and told me it was my Valentine treat. I must say I was pleasantly surprised – being driven around blindfolded in the back of a Transit van is possibly the most romantic thing Stephen's ever done, although it does make writing a diary a little awkward.

After what seemed like six or seven hours and a series of uncomfortable questions from the garage owner, the waitress at the Little Chef and the police, the van finally reached its destination. I felt my blindfold being untied and I blinked at Stephen's beaming face. Once he'd finally moved it out of the way, I stared through the windscreen in disbelief. My little plan had worked! There it was in front of my very eyes, peeping over the roof of our small hotel – the Eiffel Tower! And I hadn't even had to hit him around the head.

The Hotel Aznavour is delightful – terribly French, *bien sûr*! The walls are adorned with paintings of the Eiffel Tower and Toulouse Lautrec prints in extravagant gold frames.

There's even a signed photograph of Edith Piaf – right next to the one of Syd Little. It's everything you'd imagine a Parisian hotel to be. The proprietor, Madame LaRue – a large, extravagantly attired woman of a certain age – greeted us with a multitude of what I imagine must be French kisses. They were certainly accompanied by a good degree of stubble. She handed over our key and told us that we had the bijou room at the end of the corridor on the first floor. It sounded very exotic! Unfortunately there was no lift and the bell boy was off with some strain of French social disease, so we had to carry our own luggage. As Stephen sensibly pointed out, he couldn't risk his infirmity allowance by being seen carrying heavy items, but it only took me three journeys. Our room was lovely, but a little on the small side, and I was a bit disappointed to find it wasn't en suite – odd, as I'd always thought that was French. However, there was a luxurious pink communal bathroom, or Lavvie en Rose as Madame LaRue calls it.

Apparently, Stephen's booked us in for five

nights. Being self-employed, he can take time off whenever he likes. That'll be 26 days this year, now. I must admit I was a little worried about the children being left on their own in the house but Stephen reassured me that he'd renewed our contents insurance and besides, they'd be fully occupied taking care of the baby.

11 Friday

How wonderful to wake up in Paris – Mrs Norton would be steaming with jealousy if she knew. I must remember to send her a postcard. Breakfast was delicious, although Stephen made the faux pas of ordering the full English (to her credit, Madame LaRue seemed really quite adept with a frying pan). I, of course, went continental – croissants, *café au lait* and a bowl of Sugar Puffs (apparently they're quite à la mode in Parisian high society).

We took a stroll after breakfast and I was astonished to see that the city had a beach. According to Stephen they create one every summer on the banks of the river Seine. I must say it looked awfully realistic – almost as if it had been there for years, what with the deckchairs, the piers and the long-eared French pony rides. And the Seine was a great deal wider than I'd imagined. I couldn't even see the other side and there even appeared to be a number of oil tankers travelling along it. Sadly, we had to cut our time on the beach a bit short – partially due to the distinctly bracing February weather, but mostly due to Stephen attacking a family of holidaymakers with his deckchair after their two-year-old trod on his sandcastle.

Spent the afternoon sightseeing on board an authentic, illuminated French tram in the shape of a rocket ship. I learned so much. I had no idea the Moulin Rouge was a chip shop or that the *Mona Lisa* was actually painted on a T-shirt (and topless – those art history books simply don't do her justice). In the evening, we sampled some of the local delicacies – *chiens chauds* and of course a bag of that traditional Parisian delicacy, *flosse de candie*. The French really have a way with food that puts the English to shame (or most of us, at least).

12 Saturday

Dear Diary, after years of dreaming, I've finally made it to the Eiffel Tower! If truth be told, I was slightly disappointed. It appeared a little shorter than I'd been expecting, but Stephen assured me that was because the foundations had collapsed due to the sheer weight of tourists. Undaunted, I made straight for the lift. Stephen's not good with heights so he stayed on *terra firma*, as they say here in France. As chance would have it, he managed to find a genuine British-style pub not 100 feet away, so he was quite happy to wait for me there.

The view from the top of the tower was breathtaking. Or at least, I'm told it was. Unfortunately the lift got stuck halfway up and it took two hours to get it working again. Poor Stephen must have been worried out of his mind, although typically he tried his best not to show it when I found him singing with his trousers round his ankles on the bonnet of a Nissan Micra. Despite his evident concern, he still managed to take me for a few turns round the floor of the famous Eiffel Tower Ballroom. For a few wonderful minutes, it was like our honeymoon all over again – gyrating rhythmically to the strains of an unwieldy organ until, all too soon, it was over.

13 Sunday

Stephen was a little the worse for wear this morning after yesterday's trauma, so I ventured out alone into the city, armed only with the more summery of my hats and my schoolgirl French. Unfortunately, it appears that Mademoiselle Depardieu must have taught her charges some kind of provincial dialect, as every time I asked for directions to the Arc de Triomphe I was met with a blank stare. Mind you, I have to say that Paris caters far better for the English tourist than London does for the French. Not only are almost all the signs in English, but so are the newspapers, magazines and comedy headwear. Keen to enter fully into the French *joie de vivre*, I was forced to improvise with a magic marker. I like to think the locals were suitably impressed when they noticed 'Baise-moi Vite!' on my sunhat.

Two posters caught my eye as I wandered through the Parisian streets – one advertised a literary evening at a local theatre, featuring readings by a special guest author. Unfortunately, the corner of the poster was hidden beneath another for the North West Regional Karaoke Finals. The only letters visible were S, t, e. Goodness, I wondered. Could it be possible? Was Stephen King really appearing? What a shame it was on Valentine's evening – Stephen was bound to have something special planned and that sort of thing really isn't his cup of tea. In fact, he'd be far more likely to be found at the event on the other poster! Just as well that's also on the 14th!

Sadly, my efforts to find the Arc de

Triomphe were in vain, but I still had a lovely day wandering aimlessly through the streets of Paris. They just have a certain something about them. If only I knew the French for *je ne sais quoi*.

14 Monday

Breakfast this morning was a real treat. Madame LaRue gave us an emotionally charged rendition of 'Je ne regrette rien' before launching into a dramatic medley of Serge Gainsbourg hits, all while delivering our breakfast plates and continental coffees. It really was an extraordinary performance, mostly due to her highly expressive – and surprisingly large – hands. After breakfast she announced to the guests that tonight she would be hosting her annual City of Love Valentine's Dinner in the Sacha Distel dining room, which doubles as the guests' TV room the rest of the time. I glanced across at Stephen. His face was like stone. Obviously, he didn't want me to guess that he'd booked a table for us this evening. He's such an old romantic at heart. Almost makes me feel glad I married him. I can't wait for this evening . . .

Dear Diary, forgive my tears but I'm utterly distraught. How could he do this to me? The disappointment, the humiliation . . . I'll never forgive him for this! Never!

And to think, everything seemed so perfect this afternoon. A relaxing stroll along the '1.609344 kilomètres d'Or', a light lunch at the 'Folies Burger' and when I got back Stephen was out of bed and even putting on his dinner jacket and dickie bow. I, of course, slipped immediately into the bathroom to change into the evening dress I wore last time we enjoyed a sophisticated evening meal together. For some reason, it seemed to take a little longer to put on than last time, but I believe fine fabrics are prone to a little shrinkage, particularly after 16 years. Finally I emerged from the bathroom, like a beautiful swan in a hat. Stephen was truly gobsmacked, even if I do say so myself. He was absolutely speechless for several minutes before finally kissing me softly on the cheek, saying 'See you later,' and leaving the room, hurriedly.

Stephen's bladder has seen better days so I made my way downstairs to wait for him in the dining room. Madame LaRue made a pretence of being surprised to see me – no doubt Stephen had informed her of his little subterfuge – and ushered me to the one unoccupied table in a darkened corner of the room (presumably their most romantic table). I selected a bottle of the exotic sounding 'Vin de Maison' and waited . . .

If anything, the third bottle of Vin de Maison was even more delicious than the first two and by the time my Crème Sarkozy arrived, I'd almost forgotten that Stephen wasn't there. In fact I might have forgotten altogether, had it not been for Madame LaRue's sudden rousing burst of Manhattan Transfer's 'Chanson d'Amour'. I'm not generally given to public displays of emotion but I have to admit I welled up. Then my shoulders started to shake. Then tears began to flow down my cheeks. Then I punched the accordionist. Rat-a-tat-a-tat, indeed!

I've no idea what time Stephen finally made it back to the hotel. Hopefully in time to pay for the taxi I charged to our room. Exhausted by the events of the evening, I slept all the way home. *Au revoir*, Paris.

15 Tuesday

16 Wednesday

Gave Stephen the silent treatment yesterday. He didn't notice. Tried the noisy treatment today. Still nothing.

17 Thursday

Tried the crockery treatment today. I think I'm beginning to get through to him.

18 Friday

I need to get out of the house – all that shattering china's put my nerves on edge – so I'm just popping round to Mrs Norton's for a quick cup of tea. Hopefully that will help calm me down and get things in perspective.

19 Saturday

'So, how was your holiday?' she asked me. There was an edge to her voice – I didn't know how, but it was almost as if she knew something had gone wrong. Well, I wasn't going to give her the pleasure of telling her about that awful last night, so I simply replied, 'Didn't you get my postcard?'

'Oh yes,' she said, taking it down from the mantelpiece, '"*Having a glorious time in the City of Love. So much nicer than those awful British seaside towns you and Graham are so fond of. Your dear friend, Edna x*"'

'Well, there you are then,' I said curtly.

'So you really enjoyed Paris, then?' she said, a grin widening across her overly rouged face.

'Yes,' I answered. 'Of course. Why wouldn't I? It's the most beautiful city in the world.'

'Is that right?' she said chirpily.

And then she showed me.

The postmark.

Clear as day. Well, almost.

BLACKPOO

Honestly! I haven't been so humiliated since Monday. I grabbed the card and Mrs Norton's holiday gift, a stick of authentic Parisian rock (I'm beginning to think even that may not be genuine now) and charged straight back home.

I confronted Stephen with the evidence and under extreme duress he was forced to admit it. I'm not proud of my methods, but I had no choice. I'd hit rock bottom.

20 Sunday

Visited Stephen in hospital this morning. The surgeons were able to remove it successfully, although they had to break it in several places first. I knew it. Blackpool all the way through.

21 Monday

Can't be bothered to cook today so it's frozen lasagne. I'm sure the kids won't mind – they've got strong teeth.

22 Tuesday

Stephen finally admitted he was in the wrong today. He even gave me an apology gift – a jigsaw of two babies sitting in a big plant pot. I had to forgive him. What else could I do? I'm a sucker for jigsaws. And plant pots. Besides, there was a note inside. It simply said: 'You complete me.' Beautiful.

23 Wednesday

Made Stephen's jigsaw. There was a piece missing.

24 Thursday

Decided I need something to occupy my mind so I'm finally going to clear out the attic this weekend. I haven't been up there since I inherited this house from my dear great-grandmother, although Stephen used to be up there all the time before he got his shed. I'd start today but Stephen's taken the ladder on his window-cleaning round – apparently he lost the other one. In a game of poker.

25 Friday

Stephen spent the evening in the Dog & Duck, crawling home around midnight. Unusually,

I had a lovely, undisturbed night's rest. Stephen was asleep as soon as the pillow hit his head.

26 Saturday

Spent a good five hours rummaging around in the attic. Once I'd finally negotiated the dust, cobwebs and back issues of *Ladybitz Monthly*, it was quite an eye-opener. My first find was a huge, ancient portrait of someone I assume was Stephen's great-grandfather, although he's never mentioned him. Whoever it was looked almost identical to Stephen, only 50 years older. Fifty years and five hours by the time I'd finished up there, oddly . . .

I also stumbled across a few hundred metres of toy train and Scalextric track, countless marbles, several fingerless Action Men and dozens of Panini sticker albums, but the most exciting find of all was a large wooden chest. It was sitting in the corner of the attic, beneath a pile of Bay City Rollers albums and a space hopper and clearly hadn't been touched for decades. I wondered what on earth could be inside. Could it contain a hoard of valuable antiques, a body – or something more sinister? Sadly, I didn't get the opportunity to find out as pandemonium erupted from downstairs. Strange, as Brangelina's pandemonium lessons are normally on Wednesdays.

27 Sunday

Successfully managed to evade Stephen's Sunday morning fumblings and shot straight up to the attic again to see what I might discover inside that old chest. The lock was rusted over but one swift blow from Stephen's collector's edition double O gauge Flying Scotsman was enough to open it.

I peered excitedly inside and saw an extraordinary collection within – bundles of letters, photographs, all kinds of official-looking documents. I spent the next few hours poring over the contents. Some were mundane – a gas bill, a gin receipt, a quarterly bill from the local brothel. Others, romantic – a selection of love letters took me back to Stephen's and my own exchanges. (To this day, Stephen keeps my adolescent outpourings in a shoebox under the bed and I keep his on the cigarette packet he scrawled it on.) And yet others far sadder – I enclose a copy of the message my great-grandmother received in 1916 from the Ministry of Defence, composed by renowned wartime greeting card poet, Gettwell Sassoon.

It must have been a frightful wrench,
To hear your hubby's in the trench.
Imagining such dreadful scenes
Like being blown to smithereens,

Or falling prey to sniper fire,
Entangled, screaming, in barbed wire,
Or flailing wildly in the mud,
While spattered in his comrades' blood.

So, joyfully this card we send
To bring your worries to an end,

Let doubts depart your pretty head,
Your husband Reginald is dead.

I have to admit to the odd tear on reading that. Fortunately, Stephen's cycling proficiency certificate was in a box nearby and proved surprisingly absorbent. All in all, it was an astonishing find. To think of so much of my family history just sitting up here undisturbed for almost a century. It was at the same time exhilarating and exhausting. So revealing and yet so many questions unanswered. Who was this mysterious 'Victoria' my great-grandmother referred to in her diary as 'biological Mama'? What was the Gentlemen's Hellfire and Dominoes Club, whose badge was embroidered on my great-grandfather's cravat? How much would it all fetch on eBay? I resolved there and then to find out more, and so tomorrow I shall head straight to the municipal library to see what, if anything, I can discover.

28 Monday

Library closed. How frustrating! Will have to go tomorrow instead (between 2 and 2.30, apparently).

Fish and chips for dinner tonight. With a bottle of Tizer. Stephen and I may not have much, but we'll always have Blackpool.

March

1 Tuesday

The library was unusually busy this afternoon. Local children's author Brian de Sade was reading from his new book, *Daddy's From Mars, Mummy's From Venus*. It was a big surprise to see him there, particularly after last year's reading of *The Very Horny Caterpillar* and his creative use of the hole on page 12.

It was a little difficult to concentrate with hordes of screaming children running up and down between the shelves, many of them mine, but Mrs Blessed, the librarian, was terribly helpful. She took me to a small archive viewing room where the library stores over a hundred years of the local paper, the *Local Gazette*.

It was fascinating, leafing through the dusty sheets. Evocative headlines shouted out tales throughout history – 'Local Man Feared Drowned In *Titanic* Disaster', 'Local Man Loses Limb In Freak Soda Syphon Accident', 'Local Man Savaged By Ocelot'. I began to wonder just who this poor, unfortunate chap was. I spent a hugely enjoyable hour reading through all the stories of death and destruction, but sadly there was nothing to help me on my quest. However, Mrs Blessed did suggest that the local church records might be of some use, so I'll take a trip there later in the week to see what I can discover.

2 Wednesday

Went round to see how Mrs Biggins is bearing up. Her cosmetic surgery may have gone dreadfully wrong but at least she's smiling on the inside.

3 Thursday

Popped along to St Barnabas' Church, or TGI Sunday as it's been rebranded to attract new members. Reverend Timberlake kindly took time from choirboy practice to show me the church register. It was an enormous leatherbound tome, with entries stretching back to the Middle Ages. I scanned the heavy pages keenly but nothing jumped out at me, except Reverend Timberlake who had mistaken me for a choirboy. I trudged disconsolately home, none the wiser but slightly warier.

4 Friday

I have to admit, I'm at a loss. I wondered whether Stephen and I should apply to go on that television programme, *Don't You Know Who I Am?*, but as Stephen pointed out, that's only for celebrities to find out about their ancestry, not a simple window cleaner and his wife. In desperation, I thought I'd try the internet to see what that might yield. Unfortunately, as luck would have it, Stephen had changed the computer password again – no idea why. I believe a marriage should be based on trust above all things, even food. As it turned out, it was more difficult than I'd expected to figure out his password. I typed in all the obvious possibilities – lager, karaoke, kebabs – to no effect. I even tried the names of our children – at least, those I could remember – but nothing. I was on the verge of giving up when it suddenly came to me – Wagner! Of course! I pressed the keys and the screen flashed to life. Silly me. Fancy forgetting how much he loved *Hart to Hart*.

After several fruitless hours, I finally came across some kind of genealogy website. Digupyourgran.com was terribly helpful. For a single up-front fee they send you your very own, unique family tree printed on your choice of either a genuine reproduction Elizabethan parchment scroll or a tea towel. At last, I feel like I'm getting somewhere!

5 Saturday

Stephen's so sweet – he's always saying 'I love you'. Not to me, to the woman in the betting shop, but still . . .

6 Sunday

Spent the morning looking through the Sunday papers in bed. Stephen and I like to share out the different sections – I like the Travel, Culture, News and Women's magazines and Stephen likes the Soap Stars Getting out of Cars in Short Skirts section.

7 Monday

We're really hoping the baby will start walking today. If not, we'll have to drive all the way back to Tesco to get it.

8 Tuesday

How exciting! The postman brought a parcel this morning. I tore it open to find my Family Tree-Towel! There it all was – my family's entire history going back centuries printed on absorbent polyester/cotton mix. What a revelation! I gazed in wonder at the names. I had no idea I was related to so many prominent historical figures – just wait until Mrs Norton and Mrs Winton see that! Sadly, according to this, my only surviving relative is my Great Aunt Audacia. But at least she now resides in a care home only a few miles away. I must visit her as soon as possible! I can't wait! I'll go on Monday. It's Half-Price-Bus-Travel-for-Women-of-a-Certain-Age Day.

9 Wednesday

Stephen's fallen asleep to his *Sounds of the Rainforest* CD. He's always found the buzz of chainsaws relaxing.

10 Thursday

Creative writing cancelled again. Apparently the lecturer got caught in the rain on the moors over the weekend and may have contracted either influenza or consumption.

11 Friday

I do wish the children wouldn't keep knocking on the bedroom door when Stephen and I are in the throes of passion. I'll let them out when I'm good and ready.

12 Saturday

We all went along to the Spring Fair in the town square today. There were all sorts of stalls and events put on by local groups. It was tremendous fun, although I can't say we were impressed with the historical re-enactment society. They did last Tuesday.

13 Sunday

Mothers' Day. The twins gave me a mug saying 'Perfect Mum'. I was terribly touched – not for the first time that morning – although not entirely surprised. Even though I do say so myself, in many ways I am the perfect mother – my six gorgeous children are living proof of that. Or is it seven? No . . . six. Wait a minute, 'Thirty days hath September . . .'

14 Monday

Today's the big day! The day I meet my Great Aunt Audacia for the very first time. I'm so excited. I'll fill you in, Dear Diary, as soon as I return. I'm sure I'll have all sorts of fascinating things to write!

Just got home. What a day! Great Aunt Audacia's care home, Cloud Cocoon Land, was lovely. The receptionist, a nice young man called Barney, was awfully sweet. He gave me a warm smile as he scanned me for dangerous objects, then he led me down the corridor, through a set of security doors, down another corridor, through another set of security doors, past a water feature, down some stairs and finally through an electrified fence and over a cattle grid.

The Doris Day lounge was terribly nice. Half a dozen elderly ladies and gentlemen in varying degrees of consciousness were sitting in high-backed floral armchairs around a small portable television. My eyes alighted immediately on a rather stern looking woman in the far corner of the room wearing a distinctive wide-brimmed hat and William Morris blouse. I knew instinctively this must be her. On a small ornate coffee table in front of her was a large tumbler of whisky. Barney kindly drew up a chair for me on the opposite side of the table. 'Remember,' he warned me, 'don't get near the glass.'

'Audacia?' I ventured.

'Yes, dear,' the old woman responded sharply. 'What do you want?'

'It's me,' I replied. 'Your great-niece, Edna.'

She screwed up her ancient eyes and carefully looked me up and down.

'No,' she said, finally. 'I don't think so.'

After numerous protestations and rather more glasses of whisky, Great Aunt Audacia finally relented. Her mood lightened as I told her of my life with Stephen and our children and she positively glowed as she regaled me with tales of her life. And what a life! Kayaking down the Zambezi, bullfighting in Madrid, winning the Nobel Peace Prize . . .

Then suddenly, as she was telling me about her silver medal in the Olympic heptathlon, her face froze.

'Edna,' she said in a new, lower tone. 'It is Edna, isn't it?'

'Yes,' I answered.

Her expression darkened as she leaned towards me. 'There is something I must tell you,' she whispered. 'Something of . . .' she paused to emit a small cough '. . . great importance.'

I brushed the flecks of spittle from my cheek. 'Yes?'

The old lady fixed me with a beady stare.

'It's about . . . your husband.'

I gasped. 'Stephen?'

'Is that his name?'

'Yes'

Her eyes rolled up to the ceiling, then back down. 'Yes,' she said, after some consideration. 'Stephen.'

'What about him?' I asked. What could it be, I wondered? What on earth could this old lady know about my Stephen that I didn't?

'Well,' said Great Aunt Audacia, slowly raising the tumbler to her lips. 'Your Stephen.'

'Yes?'

'He's . . .'

'Yes?'

'Excuse me, ladies.'

I looked up. A very tall, very handsome man in a white coat was leaning over the table, flashing a gleaming white smile at us both. His shoulders were broad and manly and his eyes were the most beautiful shade of blue I've ever seen.

'I'm sorry to interrupt you,' said the doctor, tapping his watch, 'but I'm afraid visiting time is over.'

We glowered at him together from beneath our brims, and he stood up briskly.

'Well,' he said, his soft American voice a little shaky. 'Maybe five minutes more. Just five minutes, mind.'

I let out a deep breath and turned back to my great aunt. Thank goodness for that! I don't know how I could have stood it if I'd had to wait until tomorrow to find out whatever it was she was about to tell me about my Stephen.

'Well?' I asked.

'Well,' she continued grimly. 'The thing is, your Stephen isn't exactly who you think he is.'

I frowned.

'What do you mean, "isn't exactly who I think he is"?' I said, almost too afraid to hear her reply.

'Your Stephen is . . .'

'Yes?'

'He's . . .'

Frustratingly, my Great Aunt Audacia chose that moment to take another sip of whisky.

Even more frustratingly, she chose the next moment to choke on it and drop down dead.

15 Tuesday

Didn't sleep at all last night. Too many thoughts spinning round my mind. What is this huge secret Great Aunt Audacia tried to tell me about before she suddenly and unexpectedly passed away? What terrible, dark deed has Stephen been hiding from me all these years? How did she know about it? And if she knew, who else knows? If only the dead could speak – but the paramedics said it was too late to save her, no matter how many times I pummelled her chest and slapped her about the face . . .

I've tried all day to occupy my mind with menial tasks like washing, ironing and bringing up the children, but nothing's working. Oh well, there's just one answer. The one constant in my life. The one thing I can rely on. Cooking. I made Stephen's favourite for dinner. Or did I? How do I know? Oh dear . . .

16 Wednesday

Received a phone call from the care home this morning asking me if I would be so kind as to take care of Great Aunt Audacia's funeral arrangements. Apparently, one of the other residents wants her chair. I immediately went onto the computer and checked LastMoment.com. Fortunately they'd had a cancellation so I managed to book a slot next Friday. It was a very reasonable price, excluding coffin tax, font duty, choice of pew and a hearse. Luckily, Stephen's mate Barry was able to help us out on that score as he owns a car hire company. He owes Stephen a favour, so he's letting us have a hearse at a knock-down price. I'm not entirely sure what kind of favour Stephen did for him. I'm not sure I want to know any more . . .

17 Thursday

Stephen's dyed his hair green and knocked back three pints of Guinness before breakfast.

Goodness knows what he'll do when he finds out it's St Patrick's Day.

18 Friday

Stephen's got the hangover from Hull this morning. Apparently it's like the hangover from Hell, but you spend the night on a trawler. I'm feeling a little calmer after the last few days, although I still can't help worrying about what Great Aunt Audacia meant. Oh Diary, I'm so confused.

19 Saturday

Viennetta's just taken another young man up to her room. I don't know why she can't get a job at Boots like the other girls.

20 Sunday

Made one of my time-saving two-in-one specials for Sunday lunch – Spamoffee Pie with a choice of custard or gravy. Of course, Stephen had double helpings, even though he pretended he didn't want any more. Even to the point of dashing to the bathroom and refusing to come out. He's such a joker!

21 Monday

Received a letter this morning from the Out of Africa Adoption Agency. Very disappointing news. They're refusing to take both of the twins – it's one or the other. It looks like we'll just have to keep them – I couldn't bear to see them separated. Sometimes I think I'm just too sensitive for my own good.

22 Tuesday

Popped round to Mrs Winton's for coffee. She thinks the maisonette might be haunted. She says she keeps hearing a high-pitched wailing sound in the middle of the night, almost like a baby crying. Funny, I have much the same thing. Never been able to work out what it is . . .

23 Wednesday

Honestly, I despair of Stephen sometimes. He's just tried that old 'put a couple of pillows on his side of the bed' trick, so that he can go to the pub without me knowing. Might have worked better if he'd put them under the blanket.

24 Thursday

Discovered the cat's worked out how to open the fridge. We'll have to find somewhere else to keep him now.

25 Friday

Great Aunt Audacia's funeral today. Luckily it wasn't too solemn an affair, what with the chrysanthemums and the fact that the only car Stephen's mate Barry had available was a pink Hummer limo. Actually, the coffin snuggled nicely beneath the heels of the hen party we had to share it with and the girls definitely added a certain *joie de vivre* to the ceremony, particularly with their rendition of 'I Will Survive' during the interment.

Reverend Timberlake's service was beautiful and simple – nothing too personal to clutter it up, such as her name or anything about her life. Then, the congregation (largely composed of my great aunt's fellow residents, who had been informed they were going on a day trip to Margate) retired to our house for the funeral reception where I read the following, self-penned poem to the mourners before pouring out the tea . . .

'Audacia's Eulogy' by Edna Fry (Mrs)

Stock up the fridge, make a nice pot of tea,
Distract the kids from fighting with a DVD,
Set out the pies and hide the good rum,
Bring out the coleslaw, let the mourners come.

Stick Enya on the hi-fi, tie black balloons to the gate,
Put the cheese and pineapple hedgehog on my best china plate,
Lay out the platters of nuts, crisps and fags,
Scribble names of the sandwiches on tiny white flags.

There's my pork, my cheese, my egg and cress,
My corned beef on rye and my anyone's guess.

There's my black forest gateau and my egg foo
yong,
I thought that quiche would last forever: I was
wrong.

The guests are not here now: they ate every last
thing;
Packed away the drumsticks and dismantled the
prawn ring;
Knocked back the ham salad and crusty French
bread,
Now no one can say I don't put on a good
spread.

On reflection, it may have been a bad decision to leave Stephen in charge of the punch while we went to the church; but all in all, apart from the occasional request for a deckchair and Stephen's snoring, the event passed successfully enough. In fact, I was on the verge of calling an end to proceedings when the doorbell rang. I was astonished to see it was that American doctor from the care home. Right there on the doorstep, his shirt drenched and clinging tightly to his taut, muscular frame.

'Hello,' he said.

He blinked as rivulets streamed down his chiselled cheekbones and dripped from his strong, square jaw. 'Could I possibly come in out of the rain?'

'Is it raining?' I said. 'I hadn't noticed.'

I led him to the bathroom and handed him a towel and one of Stephen's less embarrassing T-shirts. 'Doctor Hausmann,' he said when he finally emerged, extending his large hand. 'Doctor Laurie Hausmann.' He was everything Stephen isn't – suave, sophisticated, conscious . . . I took his hand in mine and for a brief moment I felt a spark.

'I'm sorry about that,' I said. 'It's these nylon towels.'

He smiled. 'Listen,' he said, 'I had to see you.'

'Really?' I said, my voice for some reason slightly higher-pitched than normal.

He proceeded to tell me the reason for his visit. I was astounded to hear what he had to say. It turns out the woman I spoke to at the care home wasn't my Great Aunt Audacia at all – she was, in fact, a retired lollipop lady called Maude Blenkinsopp. Apparently, she thought she was Boudicca the week before. The home hadn't said anything because increasingly regular funeral costs had pushed them over their budget, so they were happy for me and Stephen to take care of it for them. Dr Hausmann had only just found out, and felt he had to let me know as soon as possible.

On reflection, I suppose I should have had my suspicions when I saw all those names on my family tree – Louis Pasteur, Marilyn Monroe, Sherlock Holmes . . . I sighed. My life no longer made sense. I'd been lied to by a tea towel.

I didn't know what to say so I offered him a cup of tea. He looked at his watch.

'I'm afraid I must go,' he apologised in deep transatlantic tones. 'I've been transferred back to Los Angeles. My flight leaves in an hour.' Then he kissed me softly on the cheek and said, 'It is my sincere hope that we shall meet again.' And with that, he was gone. Out of my house. Out of my life. I bit my lip and stared first at Stephen and then at the door. 'Damn,' I thought. 'I should have asked him to take the bins out.'

26 Saturday

Had the strangest dream last night. There I was, standing at the kitchen sink, when suddenly a giant kebab leapt out at me, but I couldn't escape because I had a huge ball and chain around my ankle. Then, out of nowhere, this extremely handsome, very damp American came bursting through the door, cut through the chain with a surgical saw and carried me out to safety. Oh, and I was naked. And so was he. And there was a sunset. Most peculiar. I must remember to ask Mrs Winton what she thinks it means when I next see her.

27 Sunday

Stephen was being extremely difficult today. He's demanding the right to spend every other weekend with his children. I had to tell him that was only the privilege of the divorcé, although that could be arranged.

28 Monday

Received a very odd letter this morning. From a firm of solicitors, Emerson, Lake and Palmer, inviting us to their offices tomorrow. I wonder whatever it can be? I hope Stephen didn't take what I said yesterday seriously. I'd never divorce him. I'd get far more if he had a fatal accident.

29 Tuesday

Well, well, well. Who would have thought it? £80,000! Who would ever have imagined that dear, sweet lady would have so much money hidden under that huge hat? That's online poker for you, I guess. Turned out she didn't die when I was there at all. That was just the whisky. She actually passed away during the night, but not before re-writing her will. And composing several limericks. Must have been a single malt. It looks like, for once, our luck has really changed for the better. I asked Stephen how he thought we could best use the money, but he was too busy flicking through jet-ski catalogues.

30 Wednesday

Another surprise! Stephen's just told me over dinner that he's hanging up his chamois leather and bucket. He's asked me to go around all the customers on his window-cleaning round to let them know. Apparently he'd go himself, but he claims he can't bear the thought of all their shocked faces.

31 Thursday

I have to say Stephen was right. His customers were shocked when I told them. They all thought he'd quit years ago.

April

1 Friday

We told the kids a homicidal clown lives in their wardrobe today. It wasn't an April Fool, we just thought they should know.

2 Saturday

We had a family conference this afternoon. I felt it was important we should all have our say about what to do with our enormous windfall. It was so nice, all of us sitting together like that, without it being some kind of intervention. Everyone had their own ideas about how we should spend it.

Of course, Brangelina wanted a pony. Viennetta wanted a boob job; Stephen Junior a stretch limo, a lifetime's supply of Cristal and a subscription to the Playboy channel; and the twins wanted matching My Little Uzis. Hugh Junior had some ridiculous notion about a stethoscope and a biologically accurate model of the human digestive system, while Stephen suggested a bouncy lap-dancing castle and a biologically accurate model of Angelina Jolie. In the end, we decided to postpone the decision for a while and just use some of the money to go away this weekend. Stephen says he'll book something online. I can't wait!

3 Sunday

I'm taking advantage of all the kids being out by doing those little jobs – cleaning the oven, defrosting the fridge, changing the locks . . .

4 Monday

Had a bit of a shock today. I got back from shopping earlier than I expected to find

Stephen lying on the sofa. Obviously, that wasn't a shock, but there he was, sipping a glass of brandy and listening to some sort of classical music, of all things! Of course, he jumped up as soon as he saw me come in through the door. Then he gave me that big, sly grin of his and shouted 'April Fool!' Instantly, my mind was put at ease. Trust Stephen to get the wrong day!

5 Tuesday

Rang Stephen Junior's school this afternoon. I'm not happy about him having to dissect a frog today. I'm sure there must be other ways to teach fractions.

6 Wednesday

Our mini-break tickets came today. I eagerly tore open the envelope. Where had Stephen booked? Brighton, Edinburgh, Cornwall? I looked at the stubs: Liverpool. I checked the calendar. Grand National weekend. I might have known.

7 Thursday

We took the 10:22 to Liverpool. A lovely journey apart from the baby howling a few seats away. Perhaps I would have been better off putting it in the next carriage.

It turned out Stephen had splashed out a bit and booked us into a Travelmansion right next to Aintree racecourse for three nights. It's ever so luxurious. We've got a family room with en-suite jacuzzi, tea, coffee and champagne-making facilities and a sofa that folds down into a three-piece suite. Even the mini-bar comes with its own mini-barman.

8 Friday

We went down to breakfast early so as not to miss the good food, but we needn't have worried. The serving troughs were full to the brim with bacon, sausages and *foie gras*.

After breakfast we took the Tributles tour – an open-top bus ride through the city, taking in the most famous haunts of the official world's worst Beatles tribute band. They piped out hits such as 'Strawberry Vodka Forever' and ''Ey, Judge' as we passed by their childhood homes and the Gavin Club. We even caught a glimpse of the city's iconic landmark, the Lagerbird. It really was a wonderful trip down halfpenny lane.

In the afternoon, Stephen took me round Liverpool's finest boutiques so that I might, in his words, look 'a bit of all right' at the racecourse tomorrow. He bought me a new bag from Handbags at Dawn and a hat from Hatty Jacques, before whisking us all off to dinner at Mickey Hollywood's Meatzeria. The kids and I went for the Jurassic Pork, while Stephen ordered their largest steak – Apocalypse Cow. It's so embarrassing eating out with Stephen. He always plays with his food. Sadly, the food usually wins. He's sleeping it off now. Hopefully he'll wake up soon. They're putting the chairs on the tables.

9 Saturday

I was still full from last night, so for breakfast I just had a coffee and a bit of caviar on toast. Stephen, of course, had his usual full English. I don't know where he puts it, really I don't. After breakfast, we headed straight out to the racecourse, done up to the nines. The place was buzzing. No sooner had we arrived than Stephen said he had to go and see a man about a horse – him and his euphemisms! When he returned he had a big grin on his face. He said we were going to make a bet – an accumulator, I think he said it was called. Apparently you bet on a few races and whatever you win in the first one goes on to the next race until all the races have been run. I told Stephen it sounded terribly complicated, but he just gave me his Sunday morning wink and told me not to worry my pretty little head about it. It was, apparently, a 'dead cert', whatever that is.

He opened up a copy of the *Racing Post* and asked me to pick a horse for each of the four races being run this afternoon. I was reluctant, but he said I was his lucky charm. I must say, this racing atmosphere seems to be bringing the best out in him, for once.

I looked at the lists, hoping something would jump out at me. Incredibly, it did, and I made my choices. Stephen dashed straight off to the bookmaker and then to the stables – probably to feed our horses an extra sugar lump, knowing him – the big softie!

The first race wasn't until quarter past two, so we had time to have a good look round. It was all very exciting. We saw the winners' enclosure where the winning horses parade after their race and the losers' enclosure, which was next to the glue factory. Unfortunately, we missed the first two races but Stephen didn't seem too concerned. When we finally emerged from the champagne and lager tent, it turned out Edna's Folly and Couch Potato had both won, so all our winnings went onto my choice in the third race.

For a long time it didn't look like our horse had a chance. He was trailing the other horses by miles, or 12 to 14 furlongs as Stephen informed me, however far that is. Anyway, it looked like our little bet was lost until, inexplicably, all the other horses in the race fell at the final fence, leaving Hugh's The Daddy to trot home unchallenged.

The final horse in our accumulator bet was running in the big one – the Grand National. I have to say it was quite an extraordinary race. Who would have imagined so many horses would fall sick, lame or die like that just before it began? I felt quite sorry for our poor horse as he set off round the course all on his own, although Stephen didn't seem quite so concerned as he jigged up and down, singing 'We're in the Money', 'Money Makes the World Go Round' and, oddly, 'Smells Like Teen Spirit'.

Brangelina's Dream plodded round the course, somehow managing to get over all the fences and finally came up to the final one. He only needed to get over that and he was home and dry. Our hearts were in our mouths as he trudged wearily towards it. We held our breath as he leapt upwards. Forwards. And downwards. He was over! We cheered wildly as he trotted on towards the finishing post.

Unfortunately, we soon stopped cheering as Brangelina's Dream turned suddenly and ran off the course just two yards from the end of the race. We trudged back to the hotel with heavy hearts. For some reason, Stephen's seemed the heaviest. He went straight to bed without even touching his Bacardi and Cocoa.

10 Sunday

Breakfast was lovely again, although a little more difficult to digest this morning, weighed down as we were by our suitcases, with a doorman in pursuit. As we all charged down the street towards the railway station, Stephen was still cursing and trying to blame me for my choice of horse but how was I to know what would happen? Or that my idiotic husband had placed our entire inheritance on a bet?

And of course, how were either of us to know we would return home to find the horse in Brangelina's bedroom? To this day, I've no idea where she got that jockey's outfit.

Oh Diary, as I lie here staring out into the night, I can't help wondering what I've done to deserve this. How could Stephen do that? How could he just throw all that money away on a stupid bet like it meant nothing to him? Like I mean nothing to him? Honestly, I'm so cross I could thump him. But I'll settle for kicking him instead.

11 Monday

Well, that's that. It pains me to say it after all these years, but I'm afraid I had no choice under the circumstances. I talked to Stephen and I made it perfectly clear how things stood. To be fair to him, he took it quite well, considering. There were a few choice words, a few tears were shed and a few exclusive, limited edition, not-available-in-the-shops commemorative plates were broken; but, in the end, he went.

Apparently, the lady at the Careers Office was very understanding. She could see how Stephen's chronic lethargy explained the gaps in his CV – particularly the one from 1992 to 2007. I'm not sure she was overly impressed with his preferred options of Karaoke Laureate or Argonaut, but she nonetheless endeavoured to locate an area best matched to his skill-set. He arrived home eight hours later. He's got to go back again tomorrow, when she's confident she will have located his skill-set.

12 Tuesday

Turns out Stephen doesn't have a skill-set, so he's being referred to their extreme cases department, where they are confident of placing him in a fulfilling position. In the meantime, he's returned to his traditional fulfilling position – lying on the sofa with a bucket of chicken on his chest.

13 Wednesday

Creative writing cancelled again tonight. Not entirely sure why. The lecturer just said he was having a bad week. Something to do with shooting an albatross, he said.

14 Thursday

Must be my lucky day! I found 50 pence down the back of the sofa. Oh, and the baby.

15 Friday

For a treat today, I made the family my special pizza. Here's the recipe . . .

Edna's English Four Seasons Pizza

Serves eight or nine.

My special Four Seasons pizza encompasses all the very best of the English seasons. First, every truly successful pizza needs a base. Something bready usually works best, I find. I prefer a traditional English bread such as thin white sliced, or thick if it's deep pan, but wholemeal or malt loaf are acceptable alternatives. Knead together then roll out into a large circle (or more likely some kind of hexagon). Smear with tomato purée, ketchup or condensed tomato soup, then cover liberally with that most English of cheeses – the Dairylea triangle.

Next, the toppings, each representing one of the four English seasons.

Spring – it has to be lamb, of course. Who could possibly watch a newborn lamb gambolling playfully on a lush green hillside without thinking 'pizza'? However, if the budget won't stretch to fresh lamb, there are a variety of pre-packed, mechanically retrieved substitutes available from most supermarkets. My own particular favourite is Spamb.

Summer – nothing evokes an English summer better than the taste of leather on willow. But if your local supermarket doesn't stock one or both of these, strawberries and cream make a passable substitute.

Autumn – the season of mists and mellow fruitfulness. And Marmite. What could capture the essence – and brownness – of fallen leaves better than this delightful yeast extract spread?

Winter – it can only be that most festive of toppings, mulled liver.

And finally, my only foreign ingredient. A good pizza needs a healthy sprinkling of herbs and I use only the very finest French blend – my trusty bag of pot-pourri.

Bake for 20 to 40 minutes at Gas Mark 220, or vice versa.

Serve, drizzled with lager to taste.

Hint: Why not get your husband to dress up as a pizza delivery boy for that extra special authentic Italian touch? Or a gladiator.

16 Saturday

We're trying a little bedtime role reversal tonight – I'm staying up to watch the football and Stephen's pretending he's got a headache.

17 Sunday

Quite a start to the day! And not in the normal Sunday morning way. Stephen jumped out of bed this morning shouting 'Europa' – I assume he meant 'Eureka'. He pulled on his jumper and ran straight out of the house. He returned briefly to put his trousers on, then shot off again.

He eventually returned a few hours later, proudly announcing that he'd been to TakeU4Aride Cabs down the road and he was going to be a taxi driver. What a relief!

18 Monday

A big day for Stephen today. He had to go to the test centre to take his private hire taxi exam, also known as 'The Ignorance'. Luckily he passed with flying colours, although apparently there was one sticky moment when, in answer to question 17, he said he felt immigrants weren't to blame for the state of Britain's roads, hospitals and education system.

Then, proudly gripping his diploma in his hand, he drove straight to Reasonably Honest Al's used car lot, Jalopy Seconds, and traded the van for a Ford Viagra. I have to say I'll be sad to see the back of that old van. We had many happy times in it before the children arrived. Generally, around nine months before. But I am very relieved that Stephen's finally back on track and so enthusiastic about his new career. He says he can't wait to get out of the house and on the road, bless him!

19 Tuesday

Coffee morning with the ladies. As my creative writing course has been cancelled yet again – apparently, the lecturer couldn't make it this week because he was being pursued by a great white whale – I suggested we start a book club. I was pleasantly surprised that my idea was met with such a positive reaction, considering Mrs Winton's Amazon rainforest sit-in and Mrs Biggins' fear of paper. Given Mrs Norton's limited literacy skills, I proposed we choose just one book to read and discuss per month. I had no wish to impose my own somewhat erudite tastes on the group (at least not for the first month) so I asked for suggestions. Having dismissed Mrs Winton's suggestion, *Enlightenment Through Chickpeas*, and Mrs Biggins' *Sudoku Monthly*, we plumped finally for Mrs Norton's choice, *The Brown Conundrum*. Apparently it's a bestseller, although I can't say I've ever heard of it.

20 Wednesday

Ordered Mrs Norton's book online. Apparently it's some kind of mystery thriller. People who bought it also bought *The Cat in the Hat* and the Miracle Wonder Mop, so I don't hold out much hope . . .

21 Thursday

It's so difficult constantly having to find things to keep the kids amused throughout the Easter holidays. Luckily, this afternoon they're going blackberrying. And if they don't get caught, they'll go iPodding too.

22 Friday

Off to the supermarket. I've decided the house needs a proper spring clean, so I've made a list of a few items I need to get . . .

SHOPPING LIST:

1 can Pelvic Floor Polish
Several boxes of Shake 'n' Wipe toilet tissue
Cillit Ka-Boom – extra large
2 bottles Embarrassing Stain-Away
Toilet Swan U-bend Cleaner

1 pack disposable vacuum cleaner bags for a Scumsucker Deluxe 3000

Hopefully, that lot should do the trick. After all, the baby must be somewhere.

23 Saturday

Stephen's out at the Red Lion's St George's Day Karaoke Night. He's hoping to wow them with a stirring medley of English classics – 'God Save the Queen', 'Jerusalem' and 'Tiger Feet'.

Gone midnight. Stephen's not back yet and I'm going to bed with a headache. What a waste of a perfectly good headache.

24 Sunday

Easter Sunday. I must say, this morning's egg hunt was a great success. The kids found loads – Golden Eagle, Peregrine Falcon, Fabergé . . .

25 Monday

A lazy day today. We just sat around watching the usual Easter Monday films – *The Great Escape*, *The Sound of Music* and *The Texas Chainsaw Massacre*. Actually, I like to think of myself as a modern-day Julie Andrews. I sing, I dance and only today I made a lovely set of curtains out of the children's clothes.

26 Tuesday

Mrs Norton's book arrived today. It seems to have a blood-stained begonia on the cover. Oh well, I'm nothing if not open-minded, so here goes nothing . . .

CHAPTER ONE

Professor Dirk Duval, blond, square-jawed, six-foot-two-inch Professor of Religious

Horticulture at Cambridge University, England, picked up the green telephone.

'Religious Horticulture department. Professor Duval speaking. What was that, Giselle? Professor Johnson dead? Murdered? Beaten to death by a hoe? I'm coming straight over.'

Professor Duval slammed the telephone down onto his antique teak writing desk and grabbed his tweed jacket. The one with the leather elbow patches. The one women couldn't resist him in. He walked out of the door. And closed it behind him. He was that kind of guy.

Good grief! What absolute tosh! I can't believe I paid good money for this drivel. Oh well, as I said, I'm nothing if not open-minded. I may as well read the rest of the first chapter before I take it to Oxfam with Stephen's Cheeky Girls posters . . .

27 Wednesday

Forced myself to read a bit more of this ridiculous book. After all, I can't very well lead the book club meeting if I haven't read at least a few chapters, can I? It appears that this Professor Duval has developed some kind of theory that the Garden of Eden was in fact designed by the renowned landscape gardener, Capability Brown. He travels the world on a quest to find the garden with his beautiful French research assistant, Giselle. Oh, and people keep getting killed in mysterious circumstances, by a one-armed gardener who may be acting on behalf of an ancient sect called the Interflora.

Honestly, it really is the most appalling old twaddle. If it doesn't start to improve soon, I'm not sure I'll bother reading the last chapter.

28 Thursday

Today was the inaugural meeting of our little book club. Would you believe it? I was the only one who read that silly book! In fact, I was the only who bought it. Actually, it wasn't too bad in the end. Luckily, I could just about recall enough of it to fill in the rest of them and they seemed to really enjoy my retelling, although Mrs Winton did have to leave after six hours to pick up her little girl from school. All in all, I think it was an extremely worthwhile exercise. I have a feeling this book club is going to be a huge success!

29 Friday

What an evening! Tomorrow is Mrs Barrowman's divorce hearing so she invited me, Mrs Norton, Mrs Winton and Mrs Biggins on her Hen Divorce Night. These things don't generally appeal to me but I don't remember the last time I went on a proper girls' night out, and I must say it was quite an eye-opener!

I left Stephen in charge of the kids. Or vice versa, I forget which. I think it's important for a father to spend quality time with his children. Or any time.

We began the night at something called a shot bar. I wasn't particularly impressed as the drinks seemed a bit on the small side, although they were all sorts of pretty colours – particularly when they were set on fire. Ex-Mrs-Barrowman-to-be had had T-shirts printed for us all with the slogan 'Happy to be footloose and hubby free!' I wore mine under duress – and a cardigan. They were a ghastly cherry pink colour – not me at all, although obviously I agreed with the sentiment.

From there we attended a number of establishments, none of which was exactly my cup of tea, but the highlight of the evening was undoubtedly at the end. Ex-Mrs-Barrowman-to-be had booked tickets to see Arnold Askew, the world's second best ventriloquial clairvoyant. It was quite a show! The arena was shaking to the rafters as he bounced onto the stage accompanied by thumping rock music, multi-coloured pyrotechnics and his spirit guide, Mr Pebbles.

Now, I have to say that in general I'm fairly sceptical when it comes to these things – my own Aunt Margaret, also known as Madame Jalfrezi, was herself convicted on three counts of obtaining money under false pretences after the infamous Clerkenwell pet seance. However, I don't know whether it was his reassuring manner, his trustworthy eyes or his rotating bow tie, but I have to say he was thoroughly convincing. From the moment he raised his arms to the ceiling and cried tearfully, 'Can you hear me, Mother?' I was sold.

We gasped in amazement as Marilyn Monroe's voice came from that little penguin's beak, we thrilled as Eleanor Roosevelt spoke to us while he drank a glass of water and Elvis Presley while he ate a cheeseburger. Then came the highlight of the show. Mr Askew asked the audience for questions for their loved ones now 'on the other side'. Mrs Winton was straight in there – she wanted her father to tell her what it was like in heaven. Apparently, it was wonderful – he spent his days enjoying something called a gottle of geer. Via Mr Pebbles, the spirits happily supplied answers to any question fired at them. Then a sudden thought occurred to me. Before I knew what I was doing, my hand shot up.

'Yes?' said Mr Pebbles. 'A kestion frong the lagy in the thirg row?'

'Er . . . yes. I have a question for my Great Aunt Audacia . . . I mean Maude Blenkinsopp,' I said. 'Could you please tell me . . . what's wrong with my Stephen?'

I'm afraid my head's spinning too much to write any more tonight, oh Diary. And not only from the absinthe & Red Bulls.

30 Saturday

Woke up this morning shaking. I had two Alka-Seltzers and went back to bed.

Woke up this afternoon still shaking. Not because of a hangover, but because of the information that old lady's voice had given me last night. Her strident words are echoing around my head right now, just as they echoed around the Bacardi Breezer Arena last night.

Who would have thought it? After 16 years of marriage, the thought had never even occurred to me. My Stephen? I can't believe it, but it must be true. I heard it straight from the penguin's mouth.

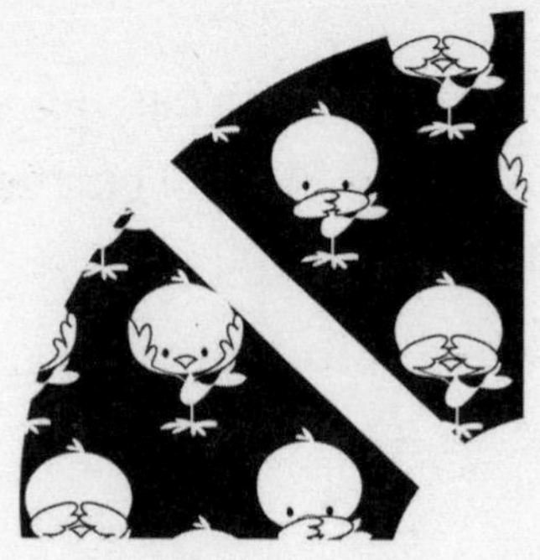
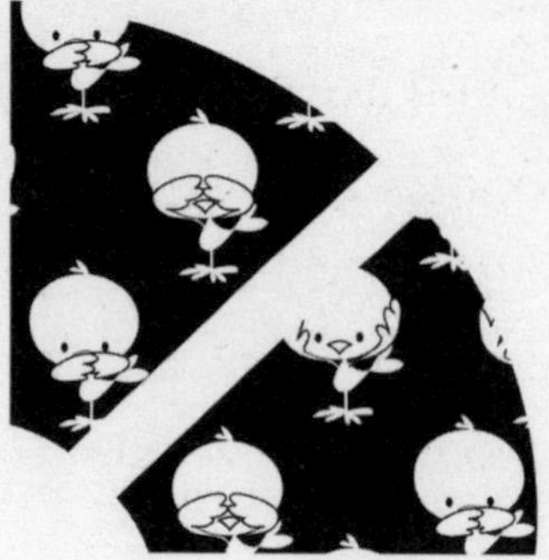

May

1 Sunday

It's no use! I can't keep it bottled up any longer. I've been worried sick ever since Friday night. I'm going to have to confront Stephen about Maude Blenkinsopp's terrible revelation. I'll do it after lunch. I can't abide marriage-threatening confrontations on an empty stomach . . .

Well, that was traumatic. I hope I never have to go through a conversation like that again. Stephen claimed he didn't have a clue what I was talking about, particularly the bit about the penguin. He repeatedly denied the accusation, but in the end he was grudgingly forced to admit it.

I still can't believe it. My own husband, a vegetarian! Of course, it all makes perfect sense now I think about it. The unfinished chilli con corned beef, the spoonfuls of steak and kidney trifle in the plant pots, the uncontrollable vomiting. Clearly, all those takeaway kebabs and burgers were just a feeble attempt to disguise his condition. I only wish he'd told me before I bought that year's supply of Spam. I imagine he does, too.

2 Monday

May Day Bank Holiday. The kids love the Morris Dancing. I can see them through the window, skipping gleefully round the traditional blazing Morris Minor.

3 Tuesday

I've just read the tea leaves at the bottom of my cup and it's not good news. I made coffee.

4 Wednesday

I must say, I'm terribly impressed by Stephen's enthusiasm for his new career. He's taken to taxi driving like a duck to vodka. Every day he's up at the crack of noon, fully dressed and prowling the highways until well past midnight. I have to admire his dedication. It's the freedom of the open road that appeals to him most, he says. That and a captive audience.

5 Thursday

Book club meeting this morning. Hopefully this time will prove more successful than the last, with the other members at least reading this month's choice. As the meeting was held at Mrs Winton's maisonette, it seemed only fair to allow her to choose this time. She plumped for something called *The Calmer Suitor*. At least, I think that's what it was called. It's awfully hard to hear in there, what with the wind chimes and *Now That's What I Call Vuvuzelas* CD. She said it was a very enlightening book and reading it would benefit us all, particularly Stephen and myself. I'm not sure exactly what she meant by that. I do know it took me ages to find a copy in the online bookstore. For some reason it kept trying to correct me, insisting the spelling was Kama something.

6 Friday

I have to admit I'm finding it a little difficult to adjust to this taxi-driving lark. Stephen was back very late again last night. I waited up for him, although I probably shouldn't have smashed him over the head with the alabaster sailor. Turns out there's a difference between 'I had that Meryl Streep in the back of my cab' and 'I had that Meryl Streep in the back of my van'.

I also have to remember to make up Stephen's packed lunch every morning before he goes out. I'm not having him buying fat-filled, calorie-packed meals from all-night garages and greasy cafés every day – not when he can have them for nothing. But on balance, I must say I'm finding it a very positive experience. It's almost like having a brand new husband – one that I don't see very much.

7 Saturday

I've decided Stephen and I need to spend more quality time together, so we've joined the National Treasure Trust. We get discounted entry into all the country's greatest national treasures and a lovely big sticker for the car – that'll get the neighbours talking. Had a good leaf through the Trust's alphabetical handbook, 'Where's Where'. So many marvellous places to visit – Ayckbourn House, Titchmarsh Folly and of course Mirrenhenge. Such a shame the 'F' page was missing. Must have been a printing error, although it almost appears to have been ripped out. I'm looking forward to our first excursion tomorrow – Lumley Manor.

According to the guide, it's an elegant property of a certain age, particularly appealing to gentlemen with a touch of refinement. I'm sure Stephen will like it anyway.

8 Sunday

What a lovely day. I must say Lumley Manor was gorgeous. Exactly the kind of place I could imagine living in if only I hadn't married a good-for-nothing window cleaner. Stephen and I decided to take the two-hour audio tour – specially recorded information on a portable cassette-player designed to 'enhance the visitor's experience and bring the past to life'. Unfortunately Stephen got us the children's tour by mistake, meaning we spent five minutes in the house and the rest of the time in the gift shop and the adventure playground.

All in all, though, it was a thoroughly refreshing and culturally enriching experience. Next time, we think we'll try the Dame Judi Dench Otter Sanctuary.

9 Monday

Beginning to wonder where Stephen's got to. Must be over 12 hours since he went out on his taxi shift and still no sign.

10 Tuesday

Thirty-six hours now. It isn't the first time but if he's gone much longer, I'll begin to get worried.

11 Wednesday

My book arrived today. Goodness, what a dusty old thing it is, too! I had a quick browse. It seems to be some kind of Edwardian romantic manual – heaven only knows why Mrs Winton would think that sort of thing would interest Stephen. The preface says it's written by the acclaimed author of *The Joy Of Walks* and *One*

Hundred And One Things You Never Knew About The Act Of Reproduction – And Quite Right Too.

Each page carries a detailed diagram and an explanation of how to recreate the illustrated position accurately and safely with your partner, and bears a heading such as 'The Eyes Meeting Across A Crowded Room', 'The Taking A Brisk Walk' and lastly, 'The Wedding Ceremony'. If Stephen gets back tonight, I thought we might try out page 46 – 'The Extended Quadrille' . . .

12 Thursday

Seventy-four hours now. Not so much as a text. Maybe I'll check that Twitter thingy to see if he's mentioned on there where he is. Although he knows I don't go on it, so I can't imagine why he would bother.

Well, according to @StephenFry, he's gone to New York for the opening of the new Museum of Modern Aesthetics. Apparently, he spent last night at the Metropolitan Opera watching *Tosca* and tomorrow he's filming a documentary on the life of George Gershwin. Ridiculous. I don't know why I bothered looking. Goodness only knows where he really is; probably shacked up with her at number 38. What's the point of being on this Twitter thing if all you're going to do is make stuff up? Anyone would think his real life wasn't fulfilling enough for him. I mean, if anyone should be living in some kind of online fantasy world, it's me; it would beat sitting up half the night wondering where he is. In fact, I think I will! Why ever not? If millions of people are prepared to read his inane ramblings, why shouldn't they read mine? Right, that's it. I'll do it. I'll open an account right now. I wonder what name I should choose?

13 Friday

I always dread this day. Stephen's so superstitious, he's a bag of nerves all day. Last Friday the 13th he was stuck in the pub all day because they were having their sign re-painted and he couldn't leave without walking under the ladder. Poor dear, wherever he is.

14 Saturday

Spent half of last night trying to think of a good Twitter name. @Tirelesslydevotedwifeand mother, @Sophisticatedbeautifuland astonishinglywellreadlady and @Worldclasschefandculturalexpert were already taken, so, in the end, I decided on a name that really encapsulated who I am – @MrsStephenFry. Now I just need to think of something to write, or 'tweet', as they rather embarrassingly call it.

15 Sunday

Still not thought of anything. It isn't as easy as it looks, this micro-blogging malarkey. It's awfully difficult to fit everything you want to say into

140 characters. I think I'd better practise. Perhaps I could start with this diary . . .

16 Monday

Dear Diary, this is my first ever experimental 140 character entry. I only hope that's enough to relate the unbelievably exciting event that

17 Tuesday

Apparently not. Perhaps I shouldn't waste characters by writing Dear Diary. Then I might have enough left to mention the extraordinary thing

18 Wednesday

Oh dear, I don't think I'm getting the hang of this at all. Maybe it's the worry of not knowing where Stephen is that's causing the problem.

19 Thursday

Oh. Maybe I can do it. I must say, after all our ups & downs and ins & outs, it's not Stephen's waywardness that hurts. It's his enormous di

20 Friday

sregard for my feelings.

Oh dear, it's no good. This tweeting business really isn't for me. I'm far too imaginative and eloquent. A free spirit like mine can't be shackled by such arbitrary limits. Besides, Stephen's just texted and I need to get his dinner on the table before he gets home. It seems the sat nav's on the blink, which is why it took him 12 days to get to Gatwick and back.

21 Saturday

Just when I think I know my Stephen, he says something completely out of the blue to make me question everything. Apparently it's his taxi-driver mate Kevin's birthday in a few days and he wants to have a surprise party for him at our house. He asked me to help and, stupidly, I said I would. Which means that I'll be left to organise the entire thing, as usual. Still, if a job's worth doing . . . and I am something of an expert when it comes to social events – my Diana's Funeral Reggae 'n' Risotto street party is still talked about to this day.

Whenever I'm called on to arrange a gathering of this nature, I try to make it as personal as I can, reflecting as many of that special someone's interests and hobbies as possible in the decor and catering. According to Stephen, Kevin is something of a bibliophile and gastronome (actually, what he said was 'he reads things and cooks stuff'). He also likes sculpture, the cinema and naval history, apparently. To be honest, I'm a little surprised that he and Stephen are friends – from what I hear, he sounds like a bit of a snob. I can't imagine what they find to talk about. When Stephen's exhausted his favourite topics of page-three models, football and footballers' page-three model girlfriends, he's generally at a loss conversationally.

I set my mind to work. I would have to think of a theme, decorate, bake a cake and buy a suitable present. All in one day. All by myself. In fairness, Stephen did try to help. He suggested we combine a few of Kevin's interests for a centrepiece and have an ice sculpture and a scale model of the *Titanic*, but I told him that's just an accident waiting to happen.

22 Sunday

Kevin's surprise party tonight; despite my meticulous planning, things didn't go exactly as I'd hoped. In the end I chose a taxi-driving theme, as I suspected most of the guests would be fellow drivers and therefore perhaps not connoisseurs of the arts like Kevin and me – I am nothing if not sensitive, after all. I really outdid myself, I have to say. Aside from the hand-painted 'Happy Birthday Kevin' banner, life-sized posters of Judd Hirsch and Travis Bickle adorned the walls and scented pine trees hung from every light fitting. The crowning glory was, of course, the birthday cake – a scale replica of a London taxi cab, fashioned from sponge and black icing. It was perfect in every detail, right down to the tiny driver and marzipan student vomiting on the back seat.

As eight o'clock drew nearer, Stephen suggested I hide behind the sofa while he went outside to keep watch for Kevin's arrival. I was surprised that none of Stephen's friends was there already – there's usually at least one of them lying around – but I crouched down expectantly, making sure that not even my hat was visible above the back of the sofa. I waited for what seemed like hours in the darkness and silence, until I got cramp up the back of my left leg. I shot bolt upright and hopped about whooping for several minutes until the pain passed. I was about to resume my position when all of a sudden the lights came on and there before me was Stephen with an enormous grin on his face, flanked by Mrs Norton, Mrs Winton and Mrs Biggins.

'Surprise!' they chimed in unison. 'Happy Birthday, Kevin!'

I looked up at the banner.

'But . . .'

Stephen was grinning like the Cheshire Cat. It turns out there is no Kevin – Stephen had made him up as a cover.

There were no words to describe what I was feeling. I was completely dumbfounded. Partly because of Stephen's subterfuge, partly because of my own gullibility, but mostly because my birthday's in September. Still, it's the thought that counts. And I suppose the driving gloves will come in handy, if I ever learn to drive.

23 Monday

Stephen's bath night. I do wish he wouldn't make such a fuss. He's the same every May 23rd.

24 Tuesday

A lovely family evening. We all sat round the television watching that classic eighties rom-com about a lonely guy whose inflatable doll comes to life – *Now You're Talking*.

25 Wednesday

Creative writing cancelled again. That lecturer really does have the most awful luck, poor chap. Apparently, he was delayed coming in on the train when he was shot, stabbed and poisoned by all the other passengers.

26 Thursday

Stephen Junior missed school again today but his latest teacher doesn't seem to mind. He's a class-is-half-full kind of guy.

27 Friday

Just came back from the launderette to find Stephen playing football with the baby. Note to self: Get a sitter for the baby. And a football for Stephen.

28 Saturday

One of my favourite nights of the year – the Eurovision Song Contest. As usual, we had a little soiree – I made my famous European Melting Hot-Pot.

My hot-pot was, of course, the highlight of the evening, with each of the competing nations represented by one ingredient – paté from France, spaghetti hoops from Italy and the United Kingdom's very own woodland delicacy, the cheese and pineapple hedgehog, all covered with my own special mixture of Guinness and Bisto and cooked for 12 hours in a large casserole pot.

I even provided scoring slips and little pens. Well, technically Argos provided those.

This year's final was held in the small principality of Bulgravia, largely because no other European country could afford it. Every one of its 608 residents was crammed into the community centre. The show was presented by the country's leading television personality and caravan tycoon Hjarken Hagaghast, and his beautiful wife and sister, Marionetta.

As ever, there was a captivating array of musical acts, the standard every bit as high as last year's contest. Belgium was represented by a barefoot nun, whose habit was ripped off by leather-clad monks in the final chorus. Switzerland had chosen a sea-lion, and confusingly the Spanish seemed to be dressed as Vikings, while Norway had come as matadors. The bookies' favourite was the Azerbaijani entry – Sasha, a mid-op transsexual, and her medical team.

Of course, we were cheering on the United Kingdom's entrant, winner of the reality television show *The Not-Coming-Bottom Factor*. She'd been voted overwhelmingly by the British public to sing Philip Glass's composition, 'We Love Europe, We Really, Really Do'. We were all full of optimism, especially considering the new changes to the voting system. We felt sure the Nobel committee would back our own Chantelle Ramsbottom.

I'm afraid Stephen didn't enter wholeheartedly into the proceedings, preferring instead to sample the 'Beers of 37 Nations'. To be perfectly honest, Eurovision isn't really Stephen's kind of thing. I'm afraid, when it comes to music, he's got two left ears. But I've known that from the start, ever since I heard his band's one and only demo tape, 'Never Mind the Salad . . . Here's the Kebabstards'.

In the end, the contest was overwhelmingly won by 'Bing-a-Blong-a-Ding-Dong-Ka-Boom', a beautiful ballad about a boy losing his father in a nuclear power station incident. So it's back to Bulgravia community centre for the fifth year running next year.

29 Sunday

Goodness, it's book club tomorrow and I've hardly read any of it. Stephen and I had better try some of these positions. We can start with 'The Coy Glance From Behind A Fan' . . .

30 Monday

Book club today. Nice to see everyone looking far more enthusiastic this month. Everyone had bought a copy and the pages were clearly well thumbed. Although I did notice that everyone else's copies seemed a little different to mine. For a start, the title was spelled differently on each one and the covers were far more . . . well, colourful. It also became apparent that these differences weren't just restricted to the covers. I could only assume that everyone else had resorted to some new dumbed-down modern version with its far more explicit language and illustrations. Typical! Of course, I put them right as soon as I realised their mistake, bless them, and confiscated their copies. I don't know how they would cope without me, really I don't.

31 Tuesday

A nice, quiet evening with my feet up and a cup of tea watching *Celebrity Cul-de-Sac*. I'm getting too old to run around after the kids every night. It's much easier to let the police do it. Plus they've got tasers.

June

1 Wednesday

Stephen wanted to do it with the light on tonight, but I prefer the dark, so we compromised. I switched the light off and he wore his night-vision goggles.

2 Thursday

This month's book club selection arrived in the post. It's Mrs Norton's choice – *The Vicar Crack'd*. A murder mystery, unsurprisingly. Honestly, that woman's obsessed with the macabre. She even used to correspond with a prisoner in Texas. Her daily letters, poems, short stories and Sudoku puzzles proved a great comfort to the gentleman, she says. Right up to the point when he sat in the electric chair. Such a shame, as he was due to be released a fortnight later but the governor granted him special dispensation under the circumstances.

3 Friday

Stephen's off to watch the cage fighting tonight. Personally, I find it distasteful but he insists the hamsters enjoy it.

4 Saturday

Read the first chapter of *The Vicar Crack'd* this morning. As expected, it isn't up to much. Any book with a misspelt title doesn't fill me with hope. And in the very first chapter the author had the audacity to begin a sentence with *And*. Clearly a course in grammar would benefit her greatly, as would a dictionary. In fact, she should take a course in creative writing (I'd recommend my own, but sadly the lecturer is still incapacitated by that iron mask). Honestly, I've never known so many characters introduced in a first chapter! Thank goodness 12 of them were dead by the start of chapter two or I'd never have been able to keep up with them all. Of course, the murderer is staggeringly apparent, even after 20-odd pages. But then I've always had a very analytical mind. It comes from living with Stephen. In fact, I can read him like a book – a great big pop-up one.

5 Sunday

I took the kids to the local park this morning. It's got everything – a duck pond, a play area, a needle exchange point. It also boasts the 'Unforgettable Woodland Experience', although that's just Mr Jenkins from number 14 hiding behind a hedge. It was a lovely day. The sun was out and the birds were singing. Or I assume they were – it was a bit hard to hear over the police helicopter and loud-hailer. Poor Mr Kowalski. Such a lovely old man. He used to be an Olympic athlete, I understand. And there he was, lonely and bewildered, standing on the edge of the sandpit, threatening to jump.

6 Monday

One of my more exotic specialities for dinner today – Spam-a-llama-ding-dong. Stephen and the kids enjoyed it so much they shot off to Burger King straight after, to prolong the eating experience.

7 Tuesday

What a morning! I had to go to Sweet Dreams to take back the so-called 'Eazycleen' bedsheet I bought only last week. After removing the assistant's earphones, I slapped the receipt on the counter and forcefully demanded a full refund. Needless to say, I was less than pleased when she informed me it was store policy that all refunds were made in the form of scratch cards. I demanded to see the manager but he wasn't available. For 18 months. Twelve, with good behaviour.

8 Wednesday

Took the twins to nursery this morning. One of the other mothers asked me how I tell them apart. I told her it's easy – Asbo has slightly smaller ears and Subo's a girl. I'm generally right around 80 per cent of the time.

9 Thursday

Up to chapter six of *The Vicar Crack'd*. The murderer wasn't Lady Fitzmaurice, after all. She was killed in chapter five. As was Maurice. Both stabbed through the heart with a poison-tipped umbrella. I strongly suspect the singing butler. He had the motive, the opportunity and the poison-tipped umbrella.

10 Friday

Nope. Wrong again. Turns out the butler couldn't have done it as he died in chapter four, when someone emptied a bathful of water over his electric toaster. I can see I'm going to have to pay closer attention if I'm to solve this. Perhaps I'd better take notes.

11 Saturday

Early to bed with my book this evening. Stephen's only wearing his Tarzan thong tonight – I'd hate to be up when the police bring him home.

12 Sunday

Cooked Stephen and the kids a real treat for Sunday lunch this week – Gammon Meringue Pie. I spoil them, really I do.

13 Monday

Creative writing cancelled again – the lecturer had a bad night. Something about walking trees and horses eating each other and a man of no woman born. Oh, and he couldn't get his dog Spot to go out either, apparently. Although to be honest, with all that going on, I can't blame the poor mite. Ours has enough trouble with the occasional firework.

14 Tuesday

A most peculiar morning. I was out doing the weekly lager shop in Oddbinge, when I suddenly found myself feeling a little peckish. Now I'm not generally much of a one for snacks as, like most women slightly older than my age, I struggle to maintain my hourglass figure. However, on this occasion I have to admit I succumbed to temptation and before I knew where I was, I found myself standing at the checkout with a basket of Carling in one hand and a Toffeemallow Chocofudge Strawberry Cream Crunch in the other. As usual there was a dear old lady in front of me, trying to pay for her weekly shopping with a jar of pennies and a luncheon voucher. Clearly, the in-store training didn't cover 'ringing for another member of staff to open one of the other 12 checkouts' and by the time she had finished, there were, unsurprisingly, more than a dozen impatient shoppers behind me in the queue. I briskly unloaded my basket onto the conveyor belt and reached into my handbag for my money and mace spray – I find it helps focus the staff's minds – at which point I realised that my purse felt a good deal lighter than usual. A quick rummage revealed it to contain no more than a pound in loose change. I poked inside the lining and was relieved to feel several pieces of paper, which I whipped out triumphantly only to be told by the acne-ridden 13-year-old behind the till that the shop didn't accept scratch cards.

I must have cut a sad figure as I strode home past the Spam factory, head lowered in shame, bag and stomach empty. I stared down at the cards in my hand and was about to screw them up and toss them into the bin when a thought found its way into my bowed head. What if . . . ? I shook myself. I may as well just throw them away. Why bother torturing myself with hope? And yet . . . In spite of myself, I couldn't help wondering. There had to be a chance, however small . . .

When I looked up, I realised I had wandered into the park. I sat down heavily and took in the view. Everyone seemed to be smiling and laughing, from the Afro-Caribbean Senior Citizens' Tai Chi Club to the young couple doing it against the bottle bank and the little boy trying to set fire to a swan. I bit my lip. Didn't I deserve a bit of happiness? Just a bit. It wasn't too much to ask, was it?

I took one of the three cards and scratched off the first silver box with a coin. One teapot. I scratched again. Two teapots! I just needed one more for £1,000! Nervously, I scratched off the last bit of silver paint. A mug. I sighed. Still, I had two more cards.

I tried the second. One teapot. Two teapots. And . . . another mug. Surprise, surprise. Oh well, I thought, here goes nothing. I began to rub at the final card. Just one more chance left to win The Mugs Game.

One teapot. Again. Two teapots. Again. Three teapots.

No. Wait. Three teapots? That couldn't be right. I stared in disbelief. There must have been a mistake. I drew my reading glasses from my bag and screwed up my eyes. I looked hard. I counted hard. There was no doubt about it. I had won!

15 Wednesday

Couldn't sleep. I spent all night staring out of the bedroom window, wondering what to do with my winnings. Finally, as the sky was beginning to turn pink and the pigeons were ambushing the milkman, I had an idea. Of course! I waited all morning until Stephen had gone out on his taxi shift, then I went straight into the kitchen, popped the kettle on and opened the cupboard above the sink. After shuffling round the large tins of Spam, the family-sized tins of Spam and the large family-sized tins of Spam, I finally found what I was looking for. I took it into the living room, together with a fresh cup of tea and a Garibaldi.

Sipping my tea, I slowly turned the pages of the scrapbook on my lap, heavy with pictures cut from magazines and dreams from a 10-year-old's head. I realised I hadn't looked at it all year. Must have been a better one than usual. Each page bore a title, written in enthusiastic, youthful script – My House, My Family, etc – together with a picture, either one of my own childish (though accomplished) illustrations or a photograph taken from my mother's *Wishful Thinking* catalogue. I scanned the images with a wistful smile on my face. What a hopelessly naive little thing I used to be. An indoor swimming pool? A stable? A husband mowing the lawn? Sheer fantasy! Still, maybe there would be something in there that could help me decide what to do with my £1,000 . . .

I turned to the My Husband page and sighed. There he stood, my 10-year-old mind's vision of the ideal mate – bronzed, clean-shaven, sunglasses perched on top of his immaculate golden hair, blazer hanging casually over his shoulder. A man with a clear sense of purpose. You could tell from the way both he and his friend were pointing into the distance. I sighed and thought of my Stephen. Perhaps he wasn't perfect, but he was better than most. Well, some. Well, Lighter Fluid Larry at least. I gazed across the room at the empty sofa with its big, Stephen-shaped indentation, and suddenly I knew exactly what I had to spend the money on. A new three-piece suite.

16 Thursday

Chapter 12. Curiouser and curiouser. Lady Fitzmaurice's personal trainer, Girth Johanssen, couldn't have done it because he was in the potting shed at the time with porn star and UN peace envoy, Viagra deLay. Meanwhile, Old Seth the gardener was occupied in the rhododendrons with Professor Hadron's second cousin twice removed, and Lord Fitzmaurice was at it with the lady who runs the gift shop. Of course, the fact that it's a bank holiday and one of Wendlebury Hall's busiest weekends only adds to the confusion. I'd better check my notes again. And the Venn diagrams.

17 Friday

What good news! We're terribly proud of Stephen Junior. He's just got a part in the school orchestra – he's on air triangle.

18 Saturday

At last the momentous day has arrived. The day we choose our new three-piece suite! I've looked through countless brochures and catalogues without success, so Stephen's driving me to Wicker World this morning so I can make my choice in person. He wasn't terribly enthusiastic until I informed him that I've already arranged for the current sofa to be collected the week after next (the anthropology department of the local college is very keen to have it. They believe some of the stains on it may hold the key to the missing link).

Lunchtime. I'm enjoying a passable cup of tea and some kind of muffin while Stephen paces round the service station looking for a map. I knew we shouldn't rely on that sat nav. Last time we tried to go to Salisbury Cathedral, we ended up in Sainsbury's car park. Or was it Tesco?

Teatime. Another cup of tea, and another muffin. I must say this is better than the last services we stopped at, though, on balance, probably not quite as good as the third or the fifth one. Stephen's still having no success buying a map, although he does have six Ginsters' pasties, an *I ♥ Llandudno* T-shirt and a giant inflatable Loch Ness monster. Looks like we'll have to try again with the sat nav.

19 Sunday

20 Monday

21 Tuesday

Finally arrived at Wicker World. Apparently. Can't wait to look around. Just as soon as Stephen's finished beating the sat nav with his shoe.

Once Stephen had calmed down and put his shoe back on, we tried to locate the store. Unfortunately, we were hampered a little by the lack of daylight, despite it being the longest day of the year. Thank goodness for the flashes of lightning, one of which revealed we had parked in the middle of a roundabout, another, a large hand-painted sign – *Wyckham-on-the-Wold welcomes careful drivers*. Stephen picked up what was left of the sat nav and threw it at a tree. As our eyes adjusted we could make out a handful of dark houses surrounding us, the only light peeking through the curtains of a squat stone building ahead. Another bolt of lightning illuminated a wooden sign hanging above the door – the Sheep's Clothing Inn.

It's surprising how quickly Stephen can move, for a big man. By the time I squeezed through the heavy oak door, he was already seated at the bar with a pint glass at his lips. His second.

I looked around the pub as I removed the wedge of lime and sipped slowly from my bottle of brown ale. It was everything a good old-fashioned British pub should be – assuming we *were* still in Britain. The horse brasses on the walls, the well-worn dartboard, the roaring fire, the pentagram-patterned wallpaper. It would be a shame to go back out into the rain but, as I pointed out to Stephen, we needed to find somewhere to spend the night.

The landlady told us there was a hotel in the next village, not three miles away, but that it would be foolhardy to venture out now, what with this terrible storm, the full moon, the recent rash of unexplained killings and the hotel's lack of satellite television. Instead, she offered us a room upstairs. It was her daughter Tatanya's room, but the bed was big enough for three. She knew that for a fact. She nodded towards the blonde, well-developed 19-year-old who was at that point entertaining the clientele with her oak-beam dancing. The roof rattled beneath a blast of thunder. I asked if there was another room available.

The landlady rested her heavy arms on the bar. And then her heavy bosom on her arms. And then her heavy chin on her bosom.

'Well, there is my husband's room,' she said, staring over my shoulder. 'That should be free . . . tonight.'

I looked back through the window at the full moon.

'He and I have separate rooms, you see,' she went on. 'Ever since . . . well, you know what it's like.'

As she spoke, I felt my body gripped by a cold, clammy sensation. It was Stephen. I gave him a £10 note and turned back to the landlady.

'So, this room is free, then?' I asked, hesitantly.

'Oh yes,' she said. 'Oh yes, I'm sure you'll be perfectly all right in there. He'll be out for the night now . . . hunting.'

'Really?' I frowned. 'On a night like this? What does he hunt?'

The woman reassembled herself and stood up from the bar.

'Oh, you know. All manner of creatures. Anything that happens to . . . venture out.'

The room was lovely – en-suite bathroom, bedside radio. But most striking were the walls. They were covered with an array of animal heads, presumably her husband's trophies – antelope, deer, donkeys, cows, all sorts.

Whether it was the local ale or the 85-hour journey I don't know, but all of a sudden a great weariness came over me. I flopped onto the dog-skin duvet and stared blearily up at Stephen. He was spinning round. I closed my eyes. I opened them again. He was still spinning around. I switched off 80s FM and he stopped. He cut a forlorn figure. Clearly the ale had had the opposite effect on him. He was in his 'party mood'. All tanked up and nowhere to go.

Suddenly, there was a knock at the door. I hoped it wasn't the landlord back early from his hunting trip. It wasn't. It was his son, sporting a jester's cap, and Tatanya in a crown and a pair of fairy wings.

'Time to play!' exalted Puckwit, waving a long stick with bells on.

Oh dear, I thought. This wasn't one of *those* places, was it? There really should be some kind of a sign outside. Perhaps there was.

Luckily, it wasn't one of those places. Apparently, we'd happened on the village's midsummer night carnival – according to the boy, a night of revelry, excess and celebration. Stephen looked pleadingly at me as if revelry, excess and celebration were his middle names, which I'm reasonably sure they're not.

'Off you go,' I said, wearily waving a dismissive hand. Stephen grinned, planting a wet kiss on my forehead, and made for the door.

'You must have a costume,' I heard the boy say as my eyelids closed.

'Yes, you must have a costume,' echoed his sister's voice.

I heard shuffling of feet, a fumbling sound, then the door banged shut and I fell asleep.

22 Wednesday

Woke up with a splitting headache. It took me a while to remember where I was. It was still dark. I reached over to Stephen's side of the bed but it was empty. I switched on the bedside lamp and squinted at my watch. Half past two. Where on earth had he got to? Tentatively, I got to my feet and pulled on my coat. I stumbled down into the empty pub and out into the night. There was nothing to see apart from an abandoned Ford Viagra. Then I heard something. It sounded like singing. Or chanting. It seemed to be coming from the top of the hill behind the pub. I hitched up my skirt, adjusted my hat and strode upwards. As I neared the brow of the hill, the noise became louder – a kind of joyful, rhythmic wailing – and the night sky became suffused with an orange glow.

When I finally made it to the top, I was greeted by the most amazing sight. Around a huge, blazing fire danced a troupe of the most astonishing-looking creatures I'd ever set eyes on, each gyrating, waving their arms in the air and howling what sounded like a type of mystical incantation. I had clearly wandered into some kind of pagan ritual. I ducked behind a bush and stared as I tried to make sense of the ghoulish scene. Then it came back to me. Of course. How silly of me. This must be the midsummer night carnival Stephen had been dragged to. But then, where was he? Which one of these masked, drunken revellers was he?

Then I heard it. Unmistakeable, even above the thunder and wails. Stephen's snoring. My eyes darted around wildly until . . . yes, there he was. Flat out on a large wicker sofa. On top of the bonfire. Typical.

The next few minutes are a bit of a blur. I remember screaming, panic, water . . . And then it was all over and I was standing alone on the hilltop, staring down in dismay at the charred remains at my feet. I turned round and knocked the donkey's head off Stephen. Trust him to find the perfect sofa and then set it on fire.

23 Thursday

So nice to spend last night back in our own bed. Slept like a log until I was woken by the telephone. It was a gentleman from Wyckham-on-the-Wold council, apologising for the inconvenience. Apparently, the 'non-fatal incident' occurred as a result of a couple of 'over-zealous' employees failing to notice Stephen when they were preparing for the weekly wicker incineration. He assured me that this was in no way an admission of liability but as a gesture of goodwill he would like to negotiate an acceptable amount of compensation. Of course, I said I was shaken, distraught and traumatised. And how much did they usually pay?

24 Friday

Read in the hairdressers the other day how parents these days don't spend enough quality time with their kids, so we've decided to drive to the coast tomorrow and have a lovely picnic by the sea. If the weather isn't too bad we may even get out of the car.

25 Saturday

So lovely to see the kids enjoying themselves, paddling amid the seaweed and used condoms while Stephen wanders up and down the beach, playfully trampling on sandcastles. Ah, there's nothing like a good old-fashioned trip to the British seaside. Sitting on a deckchair in three cardigans and a *Kill Me Quick* hat.

26 Sunday

Bought a lovely new three-piece suite at Ellis Bextor Sofas with Stephen's compensation. With the remainder there should be enough for a holiday and still some left over. I can only imagine how much we'd have if the incident had been more serious. Or *I'd* have, I should say . . .

27 Monday

Spent all day staring at the walls, trying to decide what to spend the remaining money on, then finally it came to me. New wallpaper. I talked to Stephen about it. He thought it was a great idea, although we do have differing views on the design. I favour a William Morris print whereas he prefers giant killer robot dinosaurs. This could take a while . . .

28 Tuesday

Spent the morning in B&Q looking at wallpaper. Stephen and I finally reached a compromise. We're going to paint the living room instead. Magnolia Sunrise with a hint of triceratops.

29 Wednesday

Just finished *The Vicar Crack'd* in time for tomorrow's book club meeting and I'm ashamed to admit my legendary powers of perception have eluded me. In the final chapter, Detective Lazenby gathered the remaining guests in the drawing room and announced that he would reveal the name of the killer, there and then. He promptly collapsed and died without uttering another word. According to a footnote, the author apparently decided not to reveal the murderer's identity because 'it was so blindingly obvious, to do so would be an insult to the reader'. How ludicrous! If I can't figure out who it is, what chance does anyone else have? Especially those three literary dimwits!

30 Thursday

Book club this morning. Don't think I'll bother going again.

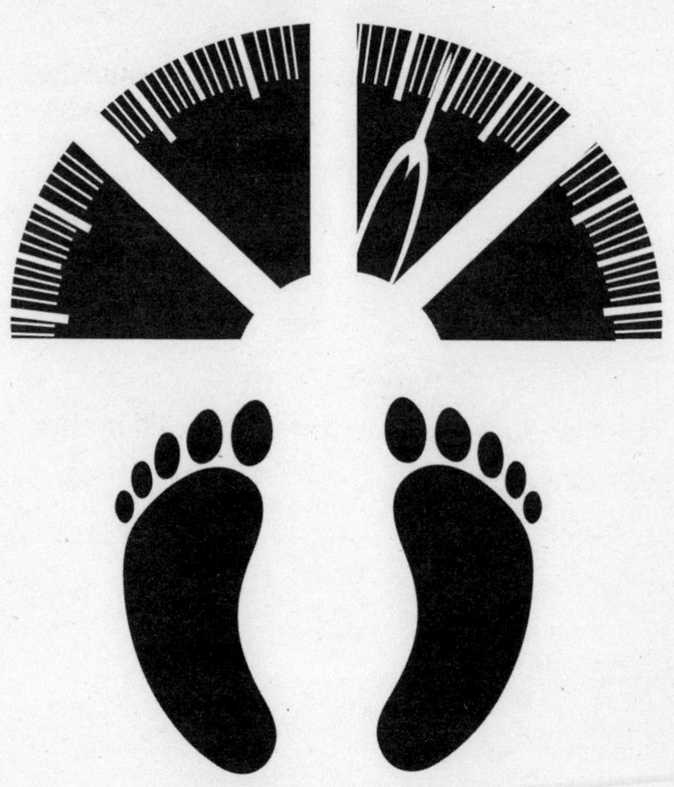

July

1 Friday

It's end-of-year photo day, so the kids have all gone off to school this morning looking even more immaculate than usual – hair brushed, ties neatly knotted, tattoos covered. This year, Long Range Len is offering a variety of options – there's the panoramic view, the soft focus for the more aesthetically challenged pupils, and his personal favourite – the unposed, infra-red special. As usual, we're just going for the cheapest in the range – the mouth open, eyes closed option.

2 Saturday

Weekend mornings just aren't the same without Stephen. They're so much quieter and less sweaty. Goodness only knows who needs a cab at this time on a Saturday. And when he's not driving, he's in that shed of his. I barely see him at all these days. There's no doubt about it, we need a holiday. Preferably together, this time. And preferably to the actual destination.

3 Sunday

Discussed my thoughts about a holiday with Stephen when he finally showed his face this afternoon. At first he seemed oddly reluctant, but after a little consideration he said it 'might be good to get away from it all' for a couple of weeks. Get away from just what, exactly, I have no idea, as all he does all day is drive around without a care in the world – or a needle in the speedometer.

Of course, booking a holiday is inevitably a compromise when you're a family of eight. Or is it nine? If only they'd stand still long enough for me to count them. It can be extremely difficult to find a destination to suit everyone's tastes, and it doesn't help that Stephen has never been much of a traveller. He prefers the British way of life – curry, vodka and karaoke – whereas I'm far more adventurous. I like nothing better than to wander carefree down a cobbled street, exchanging greetings with villagers in their own tongue, sampling the local cuisine, however dreadful, and bartering with an artisan for a hand-painted vase or gin and tonic.

And then there are the children to consider. They need to be entertained – or so the guide says – ideally, 24 hours a day. We keep quite a range of travel brochures in the house, mainly because without them the only things on the bookshelf would be Stephen's battery-operated Joe Pasquale doll and the *Encyclopaedia of Meat* he received when he joined the Kebab of the Month Club. (I have to keep all the real books in a locked cupboard otherwise Stephen gets terribly anxious.)

After a great deal of discussion, we settled on the Mediterranean island of Stelios. We've booked a fortnight in the Socks 'n' Sandals resort on the east coast. And the west coast. And the north and south coasts. In fact, it occupies the entire island, ensuring visitors 'never have to face the inconvenience of encountering the indigenous population during their stay in paradise'. Fortunately there's a regular ferry service to the mainland to satisfy my wanderlust, a water park to keep the children amused and a lager park to keep Stephen amused.

Stephen's booked us an all-inclusive family room. He says it will be nice for me not to have to slave over a hot oven for a change. I expect he's right, although I'm sure that after two weeks without my culinary masterpieces, the whole family will be begging me to pick up my tin opener again. I must say, the hotel looks rather nice. Each room boasts an unobstructed view of the sea, en-suite corridor and a complimentary telescope.

4 Monday

Stephen Junior's teacher was off again today with yet another stress-related hangover. I have to say, I can't understand the problem. With the school's record truancy rates she rarely has to teach more than 10 children at a time. Anyway, according to the head they couldn't justify bringing in a supply teacher for such a small class so they brought in half a dozen supply pupils as well.

5 Tuesday

Brangelina's just come back from her school trip. Sounds like she had a wonderful time. They took her class to a new educational centre, Science, Innit! According to the leaflet, they 'teach through the media of play and fun'. I have to admit, I'm not entirely convinced that play and fun have a place in a child's education – or anywhere else in their life, come to that –

but it would appear that Brangelina actually learned quite a lot from her visit.

According to the leaflet, the entire primary science curriculum is covered – children learn about gravity by crossing the 200-foot-high grease-covered rope bridge, friction from the broken glass and gravel ski slope, and forces of attraction by wearing a magnetic suit and being thrown at a giant fridge. They even combine the teaching of Brownian motion with animal behavioural studies by leaving the class inside a specially constructed steel box for half an hour with a wolf.

Of course, Brangelina's favourite bit was the gift shop, where she purchased a Science, Innit! T-shirt, a Science, Innit! pencil case and a Science, Innit! tetanus injection.

6 Wednesday

Had a surprise when I was cleaning Viennetta's room this morning. I was dusting behind the secret panel at the back of her knicker drawer when I accidentally came across a book. I like to think I'm as broad-minded as the next person – unless the next person is Mrs Norton, that is – but I was quite shocked by the language used and the range of physical endeavours described. I've never read anything quite like it. I have to say I was very relieved when I realised it was only her diary!

7 Thursday

Just tried on my swimsuit. Obviously I look sensational in it, particularly with my red velvet bathing hat, but I suppose it wouldn't hurt to shed a pound or two so I've decided Stephen and I are going on a diet (although he doesn't appear to the casual observer to be overweight, I'm convinced all those takeaways and nights down the pub are stored up somewhere inside him like some kind of saturated time bomb, and he lacks the willpower to do this on his own).

I did consider using the project as an opportunity for the whole family to participate in collective activities. After all, we're constantly being bombarded by stories on the television and in celebrity magazines of an obesity epidemic among the nation's children. I'm not too worried, though, as I did have them all inoculated when they were younger, and I make sure I keep their fitness levels up by feeding them as much and as often as possible.

8 Friday

It's so warm tonight, Stephen's not wearing his pyjama bottoms. I don't think the rest of the pub has noticed.

9 Saturday

Stephen and I joined the gym up the road today to help get us into shape for our holiday. They have their own special exercise plan, Supa-cise. Stephen wasn't particularly keen at first, but after the introductory session with our personal fitness co-ordinator he seemed far more inspired. He even insisted we purchase her personal training video, *Kelly-Ann-Marie's Jiggle Your Way to a Joyful Body*, just to 'help keep up our enthusiasm'.

10 Sunday

Oh dear me, what a day! Poor Viennetta locked herself in her room. Of course, being the caring mother I am, I had to go up and see what the problem was. After all, she'd been crying her eyes out since she got up and *Heartbeat* finished last week so it can't have been that.

Eventually I managed to persuade her to open the door. We sat on her bed and I put my arm round her shoulders, just like it says on page 16 of the manual. Once her sobs had subsided, she told me what was upsetting her. I can't say I was surprised. In fact, I'm amazed she's remained pregnancy-free up to this point.

I asked her if she was sure and she reached under her pillow and handed me the proof.

There was no doubt. There it was in black and white – LOCAL TEEN IN FAME FACTOR BABY SHAME. *Wannabe singer Viennetta Fry was yesterday forced to withdraw from the* Fame Factor *regional semi-final when regulation tests revealed her to be four months pregnant. Viennetta, 34-24-32, said she had been unaware of the rule and announced her intention to continue as a Britney Spears impersonator, competing instead in December's* Now There's a Bit of Talent *Grand Final with a new 2-for-1 solo and double act.*

I folded up the newspaper, placed it back under the pillow and gave her a big hug (page 42). My motherly instincts told me it wasn't the right time to ask her who the father was. She's not good under pressure, poor dear. I'll give her a multiple choice questionnaire when she's had proper time to revise.

She asked me not to say anything to Stephen and I told her not to worry. He wouldn't know anything until it became really obvious, and maybe not even then. It wasn't until after he'd changed Stephen Junior's nappy for the first time that he realised I hadn't been in hospital with an over-inflated large intestine. I must say, seeing Viennetta like that really brought out my maternal instincts. I just wanted to help her. I remember what it was like the first time I got pregnant – the fear, the vulnerability, the loneliness. I'll go to the bookshop in the morning.

11 Monday

Went into town to get Viennetta's book. Fortunately, Remainders of the Day has the UK's largest Teenage Pregnancy section. I bought quite a few in the end – *Nine Months of Hell, Good Morning, Vomit* and *Benefits, Booze and Bungalows – A Single Mother's Guide*. Oh, and *Where Do Babies Come From?* – that one's for Stephen.

12 Tuesday

Stephen and I went to the gym this evening. We attended the special 'Couples' session for the first time. It was a very demanding routine – Stephen had to pummel a punch bag with his fists and feet, as I tried to pull him back while chanting the mantra 'Leave him alone. He's not worth it.' We arrived back at the house exhausted but pleased with our efforts. Next week it's the 'Did you spill my pint?' session.

13 Wednesday

The best part of arguing with Stephen is the make-up sex. The worst part is wiping the make-up off the pillow afterwards.

14 Thursday

Spent the morning clearing out the fridge as part of our holiday health regime. Out go the hi-cal lager, the Butter the Devil You Know and the entire 'You Could Be Run Over By A Bus Tomorrow' ready meal range, and in come the Supa-cise Diet Burger & Fries, the Supa-cise Low-cal Kebabeque Pizza and the Supa-cise 'Soup-a-cise' Soups (small size). I have to say that despite being much lower in calories, saturated fats and nutritional value, it's very difficult to detect any significant difference in taste, apart from possibly the soups, but that's easily solved with the addition of a few croutons. Or a leg of lamb.

15 Friday

Stephen's back early from the Red Lion tonight. Most unlike him. Sounds like Blue Suede Shoes Night didn't quite go to plan – the new landlord accidentally booked an elves impersonator. Apparently, he was over the moon to get work at this time of year but things began to turn ugly when he started asking the regulars if they were naughty or nice.

16 Saturday

I was hoping to go with Stephen to the new seventies club that's opened, A Mirrorball on 34th Street, tonight. Unfortunately, he can't go dancing at this time of year as he suffers from the most debilitating Saturday night hayfever. We've tried everything – Boogienase, Funkicillin, even a course of Travoltarol, but nothing seems to work. Instead, it was just the usual dull Saturday night in. Even the microwave seemed less interesting than normal, until I realised I'd been watching the TV.

17 Sunday

As today was such a lovely day, we decided to have a barbecue this afternoon. As usual, Stephen took charge of the whole thing – the lighting, the cooking, the ringing the fire brigade, the emergency accommodation . . .

18 Monday

Couldn't go to the gym today – it was their annual stock-take and accounting irregularities general meeting – so we tried out their home couples' fitness routine, Sofa-cise. On reflection, it may have been advisable to wait until after the twins had gone to bed, but apparently at that age the impact of potentially traumatising events is pretty negligible.

19 Tuesday

Sports Day at the kids' school today. In fact, it wasn't actually *at* the school as the field, the playground and part of the hall are being bulldozed this week to make room for a brand new, state-of-the-art, high-security detention block. Instead, the school took advantage of its prestigious location and held the events in the surrounding area. And a full and varied programme it was too:

Firstly, the Obstacle Race, which took place in the Shangri-la shopping centre. Contestants had to make their way as quickly as they could from the central food hall to the exit, putting on as many items of clothing as possible whilst avoiding the clothes rails, shopping trolleys and security guards.

Then the canal made an ideal setting for the traditional Puppies in a Sack Race, followed by the three-legged race, also for pets, which was held in the local park.

Finally, the high street's dozen or so public

houses hosted the ever-popular Parents' 100 Yards of Ale Dash. Alas, Stephen was banned from this year's race following his part in the drugs scandal at last year's event. Tests conclusively revealed he had none in his system, and this was deemed unsporting behaviour as the organisers felt it gave him an unfair advantage over the other competitors.

On a more positive note, Stephen Junior came home with a host of medals, although there is some doubt as to whether he will be allowed to keep them. It very much depends if they match the descriptions of the ones reported missing from the Military Antiques shop.

20 Wednesday

The kids have been learning all about stranger danger today from the man who came to babysit them. No idea who he was.

21 Thursday

Brangelina met her new teacher today. Apparently everyone at her school was so desperate to have her in their class next year that they all drew lots (or as Mr Burnside jokingly called it, Russian roulette) to see which lucky teacher would have the privilege. The winner turned out to be a Miss Campbell – a new young teacher from a small island off the Scottish coast. She qualified from Mrs McDougall's Educational Training and Agricultural College for Young Gentlewomen with flying colours, apparently, and by all accounts is terribly nice. She asked the children to draw a lovely picture of their favourite things so that she might get to know a little about them, and was very impressed with Brangelina's effort, even going so far as to describe her as a proper little Hieronymus Bosch! I'm so proud.

22 Friday

The children broke up for the summer holidays today. I have to say it will make a nice change, not having to get up early every weekday morning to ring the school absence hotline.

23 Saturday

Family trip to the cinema this evening. I was hoping to see the new Scandinavian arthouse film, *Nils by Mouth*, but as usual I was outvoted. Still, I suppose *Dude, Where's My Mermaid 2* had its moments.

24 Sunday

Stephen took a rare day off today (apparently the taxi firm insisted) so we thought we'd make the most of the gap between the thunder-showers and have some al fresco family fun.

I've always said there's not enough room in our back yard to swing a cat, but Stephen proved me wrong by improvising a Swingball set with my washing line and next-door's kitten. The kids also enjoyed splashing in the paddling pool. I say paddling pool – technically it's the overflow from the blocked drain.

I kept myself occupied – TV-cosies don't knit themselves – while Stephen watched some cricket or snooker game on the black and white portable with Hugh Junior standing on the shed roof, holding the aerial. It seemed the obvious option as he was already up there holding the lightning conductor.

All in all, we had a lovely time. So nice to know that in this day and age, Stephen and I can still make our own entertainment – and not just the 'special videos' he sells down the pub on a Friday night.

25 Monday

Had to pick the twins up early from nursery this morning. They'd been caught calling their teacher names behind her back. Asbo said they'd just been unlucky and that, in his words, 'Mrs Poo-poo Face must have ears in the back of her head'. Honestly, there are times when I seriously doubt whether I really am their mother. After all, you do hear stories about babies being accidentally swapped in the maternity unit. I'm not actually saying they're not mine, of course. Just that I only remember giving birth to one child.

26 Tuesday

The sparrows have been at the milk again. I don't know how they do it now we have those plastic cartons. And I always keep the fridge door shut.

27 Wednesday

Stephen's taken the morning off today, while he has the vomit cleaned off the back seat of his cab. He did try to make the customer pay for it but apparently he refused, saying Stephen shouldn't have done it in the first place.

28 Thursday

Usual quiet night in, in front of the telly. I say usual – actually it was nothing of the kind. Stephen made me a cup of tea. Extraordinary.

29 Friday

Caught Brangelina crayoning on the walls again so I've had to put her on the naughty step. I told her she can stay there until her father gets home. There isn't enough room for both of them.

30 Saturday

Stephen made me breakfast in bed this morning. I hope he's not sickening for something.

31 Sunday

Finally discovered the reason for Stephen's unusually considerate recent behaviour towards me. Apparently, he found the books I bought Viennetta and assumed, perhaps unsurprisingly, that it was I who was pregnant. Obviously, I had no choice but to tell him the truth. For a minute he appeared quite relieved. Then briefly, disappointed. Then relieved again. Of course, once it really sank in he insisted on a paternity test but I assured him he definitely is Viennetta's father.

August

1 Monday

Put Brangelina's latest painting on the fridge this morning. I like to keep them there. It helps with my diet.

2 Tuesday

The kids' school photographs finally arrived today. It's hard not to get emotional when I compare them to the beautiful pictures I keep in their baby photo book. Still, that second album is always tricky.

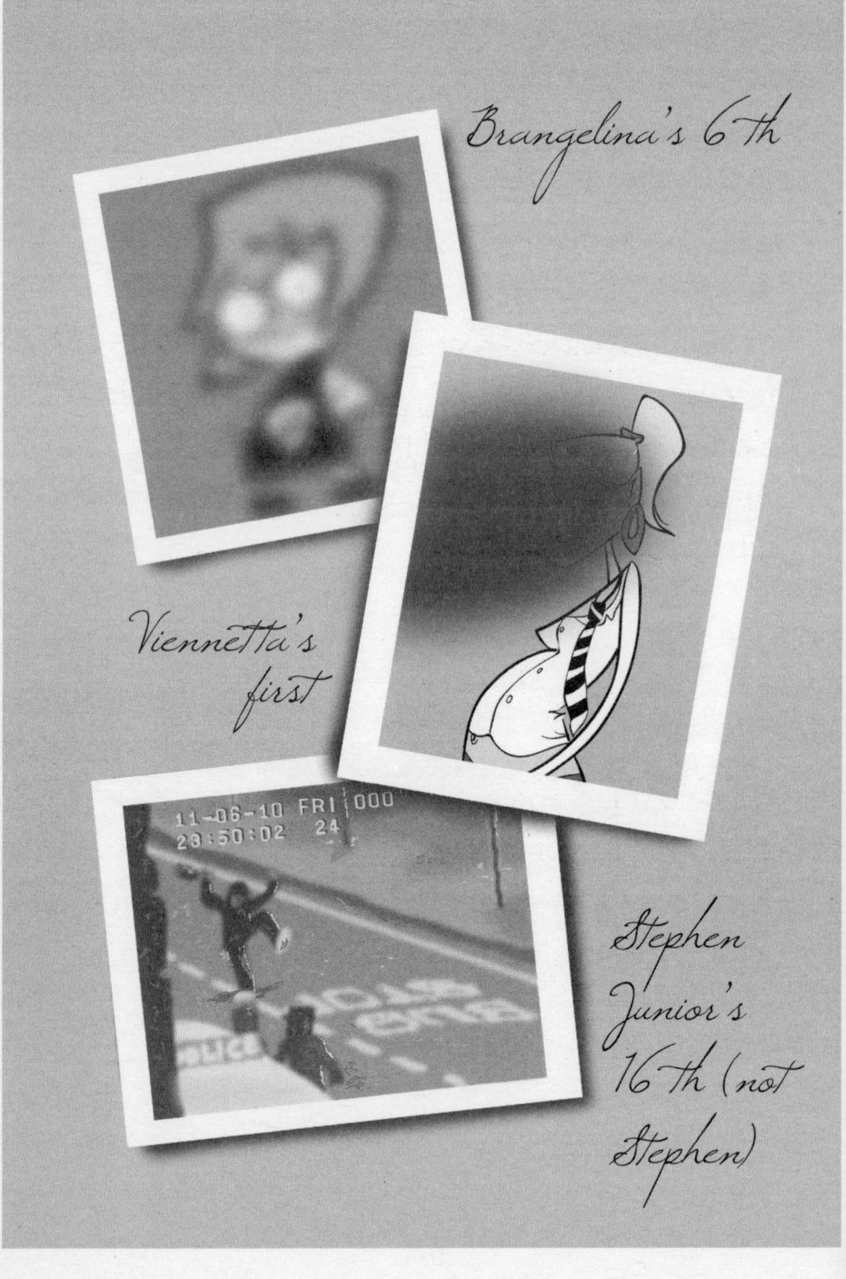

Brangelina's 6th

Viennetta's first

Stephen Junior's 16th (not Stephen)

3 Wednesday

Honestly, since the kids have been on holiday, they've done nothing but sit around all day watching the cartoon channel. Today there's a back-to-back marathon of their favourite show, *Shock and Awww!* According to the TV guide, it features the 'hilarious adventures of a 2,000-volt electric eel and his loveable bunny pals'. Apparently, today's episodes cover loveable bunny pals one to 35.

4 Thursday

Oh dear. I just spotted another grey hair. That's the last time we order chicken from NanDoes – and it was wrapped right round my mini corn-cobette.

5 Friday

Went to the gym for the final weigh-in this evening. Thanks to my dedication, Stephen has reached his holiday target with ease, as have I. Although only after I was forced to remove my hat, revealing the bar of chocolate and slice of bacon beneath. I was mortified, but Stephen just grinned at me. I shouldn't have been surprised. He's always liked a woman with a bit of meat on her.

6 Saturday

Ordered our holiday clothes today from BuyCurious. It's a website where you bid against other customers for mystery items. You can pick up some real bargains if you're prepared to take a chance. Last year, I managed to get two pairs of Bermuda shorts, half a dozen T-shirts and a David Hasselhoff toothbrush holder for under £10.

7 Sunday

Goodness, what a heatwave we're having! As usual, Stephen's wandering around everywhere wearing a knotted handkerchief. Really, it's so embarrassing. It wouldn't be quite so bad if it were on his head.

8 Monday

Stephen and I were forced to ring the council this morning. This hosepipe ban's starting to seriously affect our leisure time. Goodness knows what it must be like for people with lawns.

9 Tuesday

As much as I'm looking forward to our holiday, I have to admit I don't really enjoy the packing. It's such a chore trying to cram as much as possible into a small suitcase. Then there's the inevitable bouncing up and down on the lid. And Stephen sulking when I ask him to stop doing it while I'm trying to pack.

Knowing exactly what to pack is the great trick. You need to take into consideration the local climate when choosing which clothing to take, and the local cuisine when deciding between tinned meats. As a general rule I find a stout swimsuit and sturdy jumper cover most eventualities, and one family-sized tin of Spam per day is usually sufficient unless you're self catering.

Here are a few more handy hints for travelling abroad:

1. As well as being a perfect accompaniment to any foreign meal, Thousand Island dressing has a sun protection factor of 25 if smeared liberally.
2. Socks take up less space when rolled up into tight balls, although this can make walking longer distances a little uncomfortable.
3. Increased security levels mean that airport staff are constantly on the look-out for

so-called dangerous items – save time and embarrassment by leaving bottles of baby milk, firelighters and shoes at home.

4. Bulky photographic equipment can take up a lot of valuable space in your suitcase. Instead, buy postcards of local scenes featuring people who resemble you and your family.
5. Leave enough space for those last-minute items such as toothbrushes, deodorant and the baby (excess hand luggage is awfully expensive and it can be a real squeeze in those overhead lockers).

10 Wednesday

Three days until we go on holiday. The great passport hunt begins today. There's no problem with mine or the children's documents – I keep them safe in the sock and spandex drawer. Stephen's, however, is an entirely different matter. It can turn up anywhere – down the back of the sofa, down the back of the fridge, down the back of a security box at Euston station. It's almost as if he doesn't want me to find it! I think perhaps it might be to do with the photograph. I told him there's no need to worry, the big silly – it's perfectly normal to have an embarrassing passport photo. What isn't perfectly normal is a taxi driver describing his occupation as 'renaissance man'. Nor is drawing in fake stamps of Los Angeles, Sydney and Toronto.

11 Thursday

Only two days to go! We took the dog to Bone Alone kennels today. Sadly, even in this day and age, rabies is still a very real danger – but it's the only kennels we could afford.

12 Friday

Finally found Stephen's passport. In the gibbon enclosure at London Zoo. It's always in the last place you look.

13 Saturday

When it comes to that frantic journey to the airport it's a real help having a cab driver for a husband! Having said that, if our plane hadn't been delayed by six hours, we would have missed our 6 p.m. check-in time. It almost seemed like he deliberately took the most circuitous route possible. And on top of that, he expected a tip.

When we finally made it to terminal three, we all dashed straight to the express check-in (five items or less) and heaved our bags onto the conveyor belt. The girl behind the desk was terribly friendly as she checked our tickets – a little overly friendly in Stephen's case, I thought. We barely had time to stock up at the duty free before the announcement came over the tannoy that our flight was boarding.

I'm writing this on the plane, which is about to take off. As we all took up our seats, I have to admit I felt a little apprehensive. Not that I have a fear of flying or anything like that. That would be ridiculous for a seasoned traveller such as myself. Still, there's nothing wrong with the odd miniature gin to steady the nerves. No, I'm concerned that Stephen's usual boorish behaviour might further increase at altitude, especially with the in-flight drinks. I know I will have to keep a very close eye on him in case it looks like anything untoward might occur.

14 Sunday

15 Monday

Woke up with the most awful headache, dry mouth and feeling disorientated. Must be jet lag. I'll try going back to sleep . . .

16 Tuesday

Ah, that's better. I think. Although I can't say I'm particularly impressed with this hotel room. It's awfully bare and the bed is rock hard. And as for that bucket in the corner! I can only say the photos in the brochure were more than a little misleading. I wonder where the others have got to? Causing havoc somewhere, no doubt . . .

Finally found Stephen, when he came to pay my bail this evening. Apparently there was some kind of incident on the plane. I'm a little hazy on the details but it seems to have involved myself, several miniatures of gin and an emergency landing. Fortunately, the field we landed in turned out to be a good deal nearer the resort than the airport is.

17 Wednesday

Had my first holiday breakfast this morning. The dining hall is enormous with a huge central table housing both continental and English buffets, together with a giant sculpture of the god Neptune, wielding a trident carved from a variety of local cheese and cooked meats (and whatever else was left over from yesterday's breakfast).

Stephen's already booked the kids into the Underage Fun Club, run by Freddie the Fish, Charlie the Chip and Johnny 'the Knuckles' Jenkins. Each day they're removed from our room, kicking and shouting with joy, to take part in a range of fun activities such as Jellyfish Prodding, Russian Pedalo and 'Who Can Swim the Furthest Out to Sea?' I'm particularly looking forward to their end of week show, *Midnight Express – The Musical*.

Free of the joys of parenthood, Stephen and I spent the day by the pool topping up our tans. Although I have to say, I've never been much of a sun-worshipper myself. I find it a poor substitute for more enriching activities, like making a nice pot of tea. Just as well I bought something to read at the airport, otherwise I would have been bored out of my mind. I was delighted to discover, hidden among the usual chick-lit titles, a genuine classic – the tale of a young female Victorian biologist's struggle to make her way to the top of a male-dominated world: *Flora and Faunacation*.

It's a thoroughly absorbing read. So far, her father, successful industrialist and big-game hunter Jedwardiah Strobe, has threatened to cut her off without a penny unless she gives up her 'votes for animals' campaign and agrees to head his forthcoming dodo-culling expedition.

18 Thursday

Woke up this morning to the familiar sound of rainfall. Switched on the television to see if we could find the weather forecast, but the only channel we could find seemed to be showing a *Columbo* marathon. Fortunately, the resort has plenty of indoor activities – room service, a minibar . . .

19 Friday

The kids' big show tonight. They've been rehearsing all week. Such a shame we couldn't make it, but it was the episode where Columbo befriends the big action-movie star, only to discover he murdered his own stunt double. To think he would have got away with it if he hadn't tried to escape by jumping into that ravine.

20 Saturday

Went down to breakfast and found ourselves sharing a table with the Middlesmiths, a delightful family from Tunbridge Wells who must have arrived today. Adrian is an accountant and his wife Samantha is a chiropractor, or as they put it, he crunches numbers all day while she crunches spinal cords. Stephen found that as hilarious as I did, once I'd explained what a chiropractor was. And an accountant. Their children, Sheldon and Maisy, were adorable, if a little less socially confident than our kids, although I have to say their table manners put our children's to shame. They seemed to know instinctively which cutlery to use when – and, in fact, to use cutlery at all.

I'm afraid Stephen and I aren't really ones for

making friends on holiday. It's far too easy to get chatting with some seemingly pleasant couple, only to find yourselves being forced to spend your entire holiday time with a pair of over-familiar, thick-skinned bores. However, when we met Adrian and Samantha, I knew immediately that wouldn't be the case. In fact as soon as we had finished our breakfasts, I suggested we all meet up tomorrow evening at the Seaside Spit-roast. I must say, this holiday is finally beginning to look up!

21 Sunday

Went to the Spit-roast this evening. A wonderful time was had by all – all, that is, apart from Adrian and Samantha, who must have forgotten about it. Despite my reminder over breakfast this morning. And at lunch. And the notes I delivered this afternoon. I can't imagine where they could have got to. I only hope they're not ill – I'm sure I heard a very quiet coughing noise when I pushed the fifth note under their door.

22 Monday

I can't think why Stephen brought his laptop – after all, there are real poker tournaments and topless women here – but at least it does allow me to keep a check on how Viennetta's coping without us. Such a shame she wasn't allowed to fly. Nothing to do with her pregnancy – some Interpol thing, apparently.

Clearly the poor dear's struggling on her own, although, according to her Facebook page, she's having a little get-together tonight. Her Party For Getting Pregnant is due to start in just a few hours. It's nice that she's having a few friends round. I only hope they don't go into mine and Stephen's bedroom. We can't afford another lawsuit just yet.

23 Tuesday

Honestly, if it weren't for the organised day trips, Stephen would never leave the side of that pool.

Among the choices on offer were visits to the local condom factory and the maximum-security prison. As Stephen has a severe latex allergy and I had no desire to spend any more time in jail, we plumped for a nearby vineyard while several of the other guests took the prison trip in order to catch up with friends and relatives they hadn't seen since last year's holiday. I asked Adrian and Samantha if they'd like to come along with us but they said they were busy taking care of little Sheldon. It seems he's still recovering after one of the girls at the Fun Club jumped up and down on his head while her twin brother and sister stole his toy dinosaur. Really, I thought these supervisors were supposed to know how to look after children. I hope Brangelina, Subo and Asbo aren't having similar problems.

The vineyard – famed for its unlicensed brand of Champagne, 'Cristalini' – was enchanting. Our tour guide Shondrelle was terribly informative, although it was a little difficult to understand every word. Bolton, I think she said she was from. I must say the production process sounded awfully complicated, with the grapes apparently being crushed by bear feet. Then the fermentation takes place in oak barrels for anything up to six days, ensuring that 'distinctive, fresh, bubble-free experience'. At the end of our tour we were treated to a complimentary glass each and, while it took a few sips to really appreciate its unique taste and viscosity, by the time we had drained ours (and those of the other tourists who'd inexplicably had to leave early), we were under no illusions that we had sampled something we would never taste the like of again. Largely because of the European Union's prohibitive quality control laws.

24 Wednesday

25 Thursday

Dear Diary, so sorry to neglect you again yesterday but I simply didn't have time to pick up my pen.

I was desperate for a little cultural stimulation, and as there was still no sign of the Middlesmiths I left Stephen topping up his tan by the pool and headed for the ferry port. I must say, the ferry was rather smaller than I'd anticipated. Neither had I expected to be rowing a good part of the way but, according to the captain, it was very hard to get staff in the holiday season. Finally we docked at the mainland. The captain informed me that I had five hours before the boat left on its return journey. I smiled wearily, handed him the oar and set off along a dusty road. Hopefully that would give me enough time to explore the nearest village.

As it turned out, the nearest village was no more than half a mile away. I wound my way eagerly through the maze of medieval streets, ducking from time to time to avoid the washing lines that stretched from one balcony to another. I gazed up at the crumbling edifices, shuttered against the fierce noon sun. The locals were clearly enjoying a cooling siesta as the alleyways were empty, save for myself and a rather foamy-mouthed dog.

While the peace and solitude were most welcome after the hubbub of the resort, I was delighted to finally hear voices. Turning a corner, I saw what appeared to be some kind of taverna – a charming white building with some exotic plant twisting round its small arched doorway and a distinctive aroma of cigars, aftershave and hard liquor.

A little tentatively, I pushed open the swing doors. The buzz of conversation and local insects stopped as my shoes tapped across the ceramic tiles, carrying me to the one unoccupied table in the small, dark room. Just as my eyes were beginning to adjust to the dim glow from the wall-mounted candles, my table was cast into darkness by a looming figure.

'Drink?' came a gravelly voice.

I looked up and could just make out a swarthy, moustachioed face.

'Er, yes,' I replied, my eyes darting across to the next table. 'I'll . . . er . . . have one of those, please.'

'Very good, madam.' The barman grinned. 'Or is it . . . miss?'

'Madam,' I said, shortly.

'Of course.' The barman bowed. 'What a shame.'

I looked back at the three women at the next table. They had now resumed their conversation and were huddled together, clearly discussing something utterly hilarious as sprays of the mauve liquid from their glasses regularly shot from one or other of their noses. In spite of their traditional local dress there was something vaguely familiar about them, but I couldn't quite put my finger on it.

'Your drink.'

The barman placed a small glass in front of me. I reached for my purse but he grabbed hold of my hand.

'Not necessary.' He smiled, the ends of his moustache raising slightly. 'Is on the dwelling.'

'House,' I corrected, withdrawing my hand.

'Ah, yes.' He grinned apologetically as he backed away from the table. 'Of course. The house.'

I looked around the taverna. It was neat and tidy but clearly lacked a woman's touch. Tablecloths, the odd doily, a teapot . . .

The three women at the next table were now much quieter. They had been joined by an altogether haughtier creature in a ludicrous hat who, from what I could gather, seemed to be relating, at considerable length, some tale about her good-for-nothing husband to the trio. They were clearly unimpressed, even sniggering together when she turned her back on them to order a drink. Really, it never ceases to amaze me how oblivious some people can be.

I looked back at my drink. It combined the hue of a dawn sky with the consistency of cough medicine. I raised the glass to my lips. Suddenly, I was aware that the room had fallen silent once again. I glanced up to see everyone watching expectantly. I cast them a confident smile. I certainly wasn't about to let them think I was some weak, feeble foreigner unable to handle their little local concoction . . .

The heat must have affected me more than I thought because I seemed to have succumbed to a short nap. When I looked round, the taverna was empty apart from the barman, who was busying himself with a mop and bucket. 'You are awake,' he said, without stopping.

I adjusted my hat and looked at my watch. The heat must have affected that as well as all the numbers appeared blurred. Suddenly, I sat bolt upright.

'My ferry!' I yelled. 'Have I missed it?'

'What time your ferry?' enquired the barman.

'Five o'clock.'

He leant his mop against the bar and took a small pocket watch from his trousers. He examined it closely.

'In that case, yes, you are miss your ferry.'

'What time is it?'

'Eleven thirty-two.'

I couldn't believe it. I glared at him accusingly. 'Did you put something in my drink?'

He frowned. 'What you mean, put something in your drink?'

'I've heard about men like you,' I bristled. 'Preying on poor, unsuspecting holidaymakers. Getting them to join your harems and having your wicked way with them on a rota basis. I'll call the authorities! I'll call the British Embassy!

I'll call Jeremy Kyle! Tell me, my man, I demand to know! Did you spike my drink?'

The barman stared at me, a look of horror in his dark eyes.

'How dare you?' he said. 'I have never been so insult in all of my life. Not even by my ex-wife. Spike your drink?' He stuck out his strong chin proudly. 'I would never do such a terrible thing.'

I could see he was genuinely upset.

'I'm sorry,' I said. 'I just . . .'

'Pah!' he spat. 'Antonio would never stoop so low. I would never weaken my drink in this way.' He picked up his mop again. 'Now, please excuse. I am very busy. The bar, she is open soon.'

'Isn't it a little late?' I asked, tentatively. I didn't wish to upset him further.

'No,' he replied, mopping furiously. 'I always open the bar at noon.'

I laughed. 'You mean midnigh . . .' I looked across at the window and stopped. A bright glow framed the curtain. 'Oh, good lord!' I exclaimed. I must have slept through the night!

'I . . . er . . . think I'd better leave. Do you know when the next ferry is due?'

Antonio stopped mopping again. 'Is not possible. All the boats, she are cancelled until tomorrow. We are have the very big wind arrive this evening. They say on all of the television station. Except the *Columbo* channel, of course. They have been say about Tropical Storm Edna all this week. They say she bring chaos and devastation wherever she go.'

I shuffled in my seat. 'Is . . . that so?'

'Yes, that is why you must to stay here. This Edna, she is very dangerous.'

'I see.'

'Please accept my hospitality. My dwelling, you dwelling.'

I smiled weakly. 'Very well,' I said.

He smiled and extended a hand. 'Antonio,' he said.

'E . . . thel,' I replied.

'Ethel. That is a beautiful name,' said Antonio, taking my hand in his and kissing it gently.

'Is it?' I said, blushing.

26 Friday

Back on the island at last. As I approached our hotel room door, I thought back to last night. The wonderful meal Antonio cooked for us both – some kind of exotic chicken dish from his mother's own recipe. The storm, the candles, the local wine . . .

I shook myself. Goodness only knew what Stephen must have been thinking for the past few days. Poor man. He must be sick with worry. Bracing myself, I reached for the handle and went in.

It turns out that Stephen has been sick, but not with worry. He's been in bed, delirious, for two days. I warned him not to drink the water. He's just not used to it.

27 Saturday

Boarding the flight home, I felt a strange mixture of relief and sadness. As luck would have it, though, we found ourselves sitting next to the Middlesmiths, so I was able to spend the four and a half hours chatting happily with them while Stephen buried himself in the in-flight magazine and his Mile High Club Sandwich. The time flew by and before I knew it we had landed and the pilot was thanking us for travelling with Fight Or Flight Airlines. I quickly exchanged contact details with Adrian and Samantha (I say exchanged, I gave them my details. Apparently, they had only recently moved and couldn't remember their new phone number. Or house number. Or town), and we disembarked.

Now there was only one more ordeal to go through – customs. To this day, we haven't made it through without Stephen causing some sort of fuss. I braced myself as the customs officer asked him if he had anything to declare but he simply waved a straw donkey at them.

I sighed with relief as the officer asked me the same question.

'No,' I replied. 'Nothing. Nothing at all. I didn't do anything. Honestly. It's just that there was this storm and I had rather a lot of wine and . . .'

I was about to proceed through the gate myself when I felt a hand on my shoulder and I was escorted to a small windowless room for a so-called 'random search'. (I seem to have to undergo a lot of random searches whenever I travel anywhere with Stephen for some reason. Of course there's never anything to find).

'Look,' I snapped at the large uniformed gentleman behind the desk, 'I don't know what this is all about . . .'

'Ssssshh,' said the man, holding out his fist towards me. 'What is this?'

He slowly opened his fingers to reveal a small clear bag filled with some kind of fine powder. I couldn't believe it! All the time Antonio was wining and dining me, he was just using me to smuggle illegal substances for him. He must have slipped it into my pocket when I took that nap after the meal. No doubt he had some contact here who would find a way to get it back off me when the time was right. I was furious. And sad. But mostly furious.

28 Sunday

Spent last night in the airport high-security wing. Surprised to see Adrian and Samantha there. Had a lovely chat. Who would have thought they were international jewel thieves? At least that explains why they were so evasive. Actually, I'm quite relieved. I was beginning to think they didn't like Stephen.

29 Monday

Home at last. They finally released me, thank goodness. Apparently, the results had come back from the lab and they couldn't charge me with being in possession of a secret blend of 11 herbs and spices. It would appear that the wine we had with our meal was somewhat stronger than I realised. I do hope Antonio's mother will forgive me for taking a small sample of her secret recipe while under the influence.

30 Tuesday

Oh well. Back to normality. Stephen went off in his taxi as usual this morning and I did the unpacking. Funny – I don't remember taking a toy dinosaur.

31 Wednesday

Still experiencing those post-holiday blues so I went to town for a spot of retail therapy. My new advent calendar and Easter eggs really cheered me up.

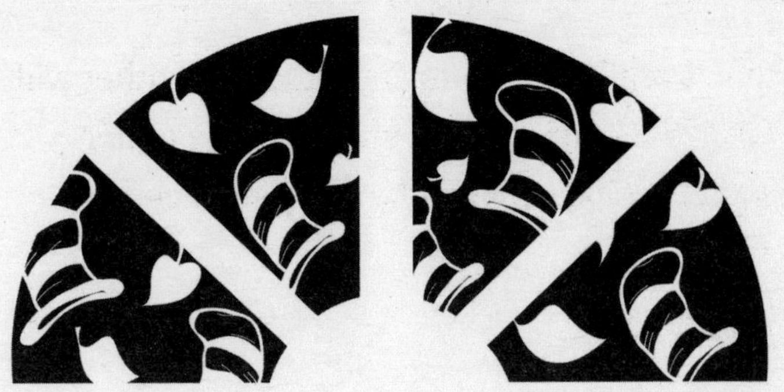

September

1 Thursday

Wonderful news! Stephen Junior's been accepted into the Young Offenders' School for the Dramatic Arts. A Fry in the acting profession! Who would ever have thought it? Of course, Stephen had to give his customary 'No son of mine' speech (honestly, if I've heard it once I've heard it a thousand times, most notably at Hugh Junior's birth), but in the end he was forced to relent, albeit grudgingly, so a week on Monday will be Stephen Junior's first day at YODA.

2 Friday

Stephen's such a typical bloke. He's just stuck his Football League fixture list on the bedroom ceiling. You can barely see the mirror now.

3 Saturday

Took the kids to Poundsweater to get their new school uniforms today. Of course, I wouldn't normally countenance such an outrageous extravagance – usually, Hugh Junior wears Stephen Junior's hand-me-downs, Brangelina wears Viennetta's and the twins wear each other's. This only leaves Stephen Junior and Viennetta, but as they spend most of their time on suspension – generally for not wearing the school uniform (or in Viennetta's case, very much at all) – that's never been a problem.

This year, however, things have changed. Not only have the primary, secondary and nursery schools amalgamated to save money (a logistical nightmare, as every classroom now legally requires state-of-the-art computer equipment, the complete works of Shakespeare and a sandpit), but following Ms Tripplemount's early retirement the local council has brought in a new 'super-head', Mr deClarkson, in a last-ditch attempt to 'turn the schools round'.

According to the email Mr deClarkson sent out yesterday, 'Smart appearance = Smart brains', so one of the first things to be implemented is a brand new school uniform. In come bright red pullovers emblazoned with the school crest, striped school ties and school caps; and out go school hoodies, school N-Dubz T-shirts and school holsters.

Which is all well and good but it's us poor parents who have to bear the brunt. I shall be surprised if I have much change left from £20.

4 Sunday

I told Stephen I didn't fancy playing lady of the manor and naughty farmhand this morning, but he's ploughing on regardless.

5 Monday

First day of the new school year. After six weeks with the little darlings, it's always awfully sad to see them walk out of that front door with their little bags slung over their shoulders. Fortunately, our bedroom window faces the back yard so I don't have to.

6 Tuesday

I must say, Hugh Junior seems to have settled into the new school very quickly. He was terribly excited when he told me about the purpose-built science block (complete with its own Petri dish and Bunsen burner) when he got back yesterday. He seems genuinely enthusiastic about learning. Obviously he gets that from me.

7 Wednesday

Received another email from Mr deClarkson. He says that having spent a couple of days familiarising himself with the 'socio-economic-appropriate challenges facing this learning facilitation environment' he has decided to introduce a new disciplinary system. He clearly means business. With immediate effect, he's banning swearing, blades and narcotics from the school premises, and that even extends to the pupils.

8 Thursday

Found Stephen relieving himself in the wardrobe again last night. He wasn't drunk. He just really hates that new shirt I bought him.

9 Friday

Stephen's just texted. Apparently, he's moved on from the Red Lion to Spearmint Ronnie's. That's what I love about my Stephen – he's so considerate. Whenever he gets the drunken urge to frequent a jazz and lap-dancing establishment, he always lets me know – very often in capitals, with a LOL or OMG for good measure.

10 Saturday

What a lovely surprise. If there's one cultural event that unites the Fry family it's Scufflemania, the pinnacle of the year's fight season. This year, for the very first time, it's being held in our own Red Lion car park and Stephen's got us all tickets for tomorrow night. Of course it's not really my cup of tea, but being the selfless individual I am I'm happy to make the effort in the cause of family unity.

11 Sunday

What a night! Scufflemania certainly doesn't disappoint. We arrived early and took up our seats on the recycle bin. The crisp packets, vomit and sexually experimental couples had been tidied away and the car park had been transformed into a modern day Colosseum, awaiting the entry of the gladiators who would battle it out for the envied title of Undisputed Pub Car Park Champion.

It wasn't long before the place was full, the crowd buzzing with anticipation. As 11 o'clock approached, the car park fell silent. The security lights were dimmed and all eyes strained to focus on the entrance to the snug. Suddenly, Sparks' seventies high-energy pop classic, 'This Town Ain't Big Enough For the Both of Us' struck up from the pub jukebox, the lights rose to full beam and out strode the first competitor to a combination of wild applause and verbal abuse. Over the karaoke mic, the landlord announced him as 'Steroid – the five-foot-two-inch borderline psychotic powerhouse from Lytham St Anne's'. 'Steroid', aka Shane Watkins, limbered up on the floodlit tarmac by punching several members of the front row as his opponent B.G.B. entered the arena, also to the strains of Sparks' seventies high-energy pop classic, 'This Town Ain't Big Enough For the Both of Us'. The jukebox has a very limited selection. Apparently, it's either Sparks or Enya.

The fight see-sawed from one man to the other, with Steroid having the upper hand for many of the early rounds before Big Girl's Blouse struck back with his trademark move, the broken bottle. In the end Steroid was triumphant, securing a place in the final with the classic 'lawnmower to the face'. There, he was pitted against the mysterious Masked Chief Inspector Bryant, conqueror of the much-fancied Caretaker.

It was a gruelling encounter, but after 30 bruising minutes a combination of guile, stamina and a set of incriminating photographs was enough to put Steroid away in the fourth. The Masked Chief Inspector left the arena holding the championship belt aloft, to a chorus of disapproval and 'Orinoco Flow'.

12 Monday

Stephen Junior's first day at YODA. It's so nice to see him enthusiastic about something other than mindless violence and Lion bars. Today they gave an introductory lecture, detailing all the different components of the course. It's quite a range, I must say – everything from busking skills to vocal projection for *Big Issue* sellers. Stephen Junior's opted initially for 'Extras Work for Beginners: How to Blend Seamlessly into the Background' and 'Overacting on a Budget: The Straight to Video Method'.

13 Tuesday

Very exciting! Only his second day and Stephen Junior's been given a part in the school's Christmas production of Stephen Sondheim's Kray twins musical *A Little R 'n' R*. He's got the role of Man in Kebab Shop. Even Stephen was impressed when I told him, although he still maintains that acting is no kind of career and he ought to get something more fitting to 'a real man' – presumably, 'real man in real kebab shop'.

14 Wednesday

Inspired by Stephen Junior, I've started a new course this evening myself. Sadly, the creative writing isn't running this term, due to the lecturer taking a sabbatical to go round the world (he's travelling by balloon – should be back in just under three months, apparently), so I've opted instead for a poetry course. I must say the lecturer, Angela Wordsmith, is lovely. She's a published poet, awfully poised and elegant – rather like a very slightly younger version of myself – and she seems to have taken quite a shine to me. I think she probably senses a kindred spirit – after all, I do have the soul of a poet. In fact, I don't know why I haven't done this sooner. To think, all those years of creative brilliance wasted. Thank goodness I realised in time, otherwise the world might have been denied my genius.

Tonight was an informal introductory session, clearly aimed at those members of the class less gifted than I. We sat in a circle, discussing our influences. I have to say I did feel a twinge of embarrassment for the others as they trotted out the usual suspects – Keats, Byron, Coleridge . . . Honestly, you'd think no one since the twelfth century had written a poem.

After that, we had a little workshop in which we each had just 10 minutes to write a poem, or a stream of consciousness, as Ms Wordsmith called it, on the subject of autumn. Then we each took a turn to read ours to the rest of the group. I was a little nervous initially but, having heard the first few efforts, I knew I had nothing to worry about. When it came to my turn, I rose confidently from my chair and, holding my sheet of A4 at arm's length, I proceeded to read. I'm so proud of my effort that I've stuck it in this diary for posterity . . .

'AUTUMN' by Edna Fry (Mrs)

I woke up this morning and peered through the curtain,
And spied an odd sight that was strange, that's for certain.
A beautiful carpet had covered the ground,
A carpet of orange, red, yellow and brown . . .

I said to myself, 'What is this that I see?'
A ground-covering carpet? Why, this cannot be!
But then I looked closer. I looked at the trees,
I looked at the sky and the absence of bees.

The trees were all bare, it was not time for lunch,
So I crunched and I munched through my leafless branch brunch.
I wolfed down my breakfast of tea, toast and jam,
Of bacon and shmacon and green eggs and Spam.

And when I was done and my stomach was bursting,
And the squeeps were all squeeped and the squirsts were all squirsting,

I started to wander and ponder and muse,
And my muse-ponder wander brought very good news.

For as thoughts are all thunk and reasons are reasoned,
So weeks are all week and seasons are seasoned.
If this were America, then it would be fall,
But we're right here in England, so it's not fall at all.

And now it was clearer than clearer can be,
As clear as a clear-clear on a clear-clearing clee!
I giggled and jiggled and smacked my sore tum,
And I jumped up and cried, 'Why this must be autumn!'

And from that day to this, when the streets are all covered,
And the scarves are all scarfed and the gloves are all glovered,
And my brunch is all munched and my tum is sore tumnal,
I know that this season, it must be autumnal.

I sat back in my seat, exhausted. I think I can safely say that the group was more than a little taken aback by the raw power of my performance. They sat open-mouthed for what seemed an age before Angela clasped her hands together enthusiastically and announced that was the end of the session.

I'm not an insensitive person, so I waited until the rest of the class had left before asking Ms Wordsmith for her opinion of my work. She was extremely encouraging. She placed her arm round my shoulder and told me that I possessed 'a highly distinctive poetic voice'. Now, I'm not one for public displays of emotion – or private, come to that, unless it's a Sunday morning – but I have to say I had an ever-so-small skip in my step as I walked home from the community college tonight. Finally, I've been discovered!

15 Thursday

Had a letter from Miss Campbell today. She'd like us to come in on Monday so that she can talk to us about Brangelina. I can't wait. Brangelina's the only one of our children who's never had a single report. Or detention. Or criminal record.

16 Friday

Oh dear! I knew it was all going too well. Stephen Junior's just come home early from drama school. He's been thrown out of the Christmas performance. According to the letter he brought back, he is 'exhibiting levels of violent behaviour unacceptable in an educational environment – or gangland London'. The poor dear's distraught, although I expect Stephen will be delighted.

17 Saturday

Stephen's sulking this morning. I refused to wear my woodland creature costume for him last night even though he's been badgering me for ages.

18 Sunday

Felt bad about the other night so I wore my Bo Peep outfit for Stephen this morning. He was feeling a little sheepish.

19 Monday

Goodness! I've just had a call from the drama school. They've decided to reinstate Stephen Junior in the show. Not only that, but he's now playing Reggie Kray. And Ronnie. And their mother. When I asked what had made them change their mind, they just said that his father had had 'a little word'. Extraordinary!

20 Tuesday

We went to meet Brangelina's new teacher after school. Miss Campbell was extremely nice when we eventually found her, crouching in the stock-room with a Silk Cut hanging from her lips. It turns out she's only recently taken them up, but apparently the new head has some objection to staff smoking in the classroom. He said the children might suffer from passive smoking, so he obviously doesn't know them very well yet.

It's clear that in the short time Miss Campbell has been in the school, she's already managed to settle in very well. She'd made the class stock-room into something of a haven, with its candles, panic button and bible pages covering the walls. She was evidently delighted to see us, jumping up sharply the moment she saw our faces in the candlelight. Once she'd stubbed out her cigarette into the sandpit, we all took seats around her desk. Stephen shuffled uncomfortably in his chair. Sitting there, in that environment, was obviously bringing to mind all those spankings he'd received – although to be fair, I didn't think I had been any harsher than normal with him this weekend.

Miss Campbell said she'd invited us to the school so that she could discuss her first impressions of Brangelina. She said she had read through every child's school record before the beginning of term to fully acquaint herself with their academic progress and any 'issues' that might need to be addressed. Unfortunately, Brangelina's file had been destroyed in the most recent school fire – the only one that had, apparently – and none of her previous teachers were available to provide their views, owing to a combination of early retirements and sudden, inexplicable, disfiguring accidents – so she felt it might be a good idea to get 'a little background' on Brangelina.

Stephen merely sat in silence throughout, eyeing the bookshelf with suspicion, but I said I would be happy to answer any questions about our little angel. Once Miss Campbell had recovered from a small coughing fit, she pulled out a typewritten sheet from her desk drawer and began.

She asked about a variety of things, from Brangelina's birth date and blood group to more specific questions like whether she suffered from any allergies; for example, places of worship or religious artefacts?

All in all, it was a thoroughly enjoyable and useful meeting and I'd like to think Miss Campbell felt the same, although it was a little hard to tell as she had to dash off suddenly. I believe she said something about wanting to make it home before nightfall.

21 Wednesday

Poetry class this evening. The title of tonight's session was 'Does Poetry Always Have to Rhyme?' Ms Wordsmith apologised for asking such a simplistic question but she clearly hadn't accounted for the philistines who make up the rest of her class, as every single one of them contrived to get the answer wrong. It was left to me to put them right, as usual. They're clearly not poets and they don't know its.

22 Thursday

Oh dear. Just got a phone call from school. They've discovered that Brangelina's been demanding dinner money with menaces. Apparently, the teachers are very concerned as they say their salary isn't that great to begin with. They want me to go in for another meeting. Honestly, I spend more time in that place than my kids!

23 Friday

I was a little concerned to receive an email this morning from Mr deClarkson. He writes that in an attempt to improve the health of the pupils and thereby increase concentration levels in the classroom, the school will be introducing a new Five-a-Day scheme. I was horrified. Of course, I rang Mrs Winton immediately but she explained that Five-a-Day had something to do with fruit and vegetables and not what Stephen has been telling me all these years.

24 Saturday

Another weekend taxi job for Stephen. I've no idea where he's driving to but I know what his sat nav's like. According to Twitter, he's visiting a rhino reserve in Ghana. I don't know why I even bother looking at it. I'd be far better off occupying my mind with something more intellectually demanding. Maybe I'll search for something. I'll try Ask Wooster . . .

25 Sunday

I suppose I should be getting to bed – the kids will be up soon, wanting their breakfast, and I really can't be bothered with all that. I just wish they wouldn't make these websites so addictive. Online Happy Families wasn't really my cup of tea – for some reason I just couldn't get to grips with the concept – but online Ker-Plunk's got me completely hooked. Just one more round and I'm in the big final to face Mickey 'the Marbles' Mulligan.

26 Monday

Still not convinced by this Five-a-Day lark so I've come up with my own alternative – Ednables. Each small pack contains everything a child requires to help them cope with the strains and stresses of the school day, as well as providing them with the energy they need – three Benson & Hedges, a can of Red Bull and a slice of my special recipe Short Attention Spam, to keep them focused over those short, intense concentration periods such as registration. I've already got a dozen orders from the other parents. It's a pity I've chosen to eschew the world of commerce in order to follow my muse; I'd make a killing.

27 Tuesday

Had quite a surprise when I went in to Brangelina's school this morning. I was expecting to just see her teacher again, but I was shown to the headmaster's office. I've not met Mr deClarkson face to face but he seemed quite a personable young man – almost dashing, you might say. He got on my good side straight away when he said that Brangelina was 'clearly a very special little girl' – I certainly couldn't argue with that.

He said it had been brought to his attention that Brangelina was exhibiting 'specific non-positive personality traits' which appeared to be having 'a detrimental effect on her in-school experience', as well as that of her classmates, the teachers and the school tortoise. To that end, he said, he and a team of specialists – including the Head of Learning Support, a behavioural psychologist and the school exorcist – had drawn up an individual plan which contained certain targets he hoped

Brangelina would be capable of attaining. Apparently, Brangelina was currently on level one of the plan – 'working towards not being the Antichrist'.

I must say it makes such a pleasant change to talk to someone who really listens and cares about the important things. And has such nice wallpaper too.

28 Wednesday

Stephen spent all day in his shed again today. Goodness knows what he gets up to in there. I know for a fact his Scalextric won't fit and his magazines are all under the bed. Whatever it is, he clearly finds it more interesting than spending time with me. Well, two can play at that game. I'm off to my poetry class. At last I have an interest befitting my intellect. Tonight, we're going to be using the iambic pentameter. I just hope I don't drop it.

29 Thursday

Had lunch with Mrs Norton and Mrs Winton. The Happy Carnivore's closed while the owner assists Environmental Health with their enquiries, so we were forced to go instead to MacBeth's – or as the proprietor Ms Bethany Hurley (a leading light in the local amateur dramatic scene) calls it, 'the Scottish vegetarian café'. Mrs Winton and Mrs Norton had the Burnham Wood-smoked Soya and Couscous Calzone, while I satisfied myself with the Duncan Doughnut.

Following our usual free-ranging chat, I hesitantly brought up my concerns about Stephen – the long hours he spends on the road, and recently the even longer hours in his shed. I knew it was a mistake the minute I opened my mouth. Mrs Norton seemed only too keen to be distracted from her meal and I was subjected to a stream of banal platitudes and homilies. In the end, it was left to Ms Hurley to give me the advice I needed. As she cleared my plate she said curtly, 'Sounds like you need to have a look in his shed, love.'

Of course! It was all so simple. I left the other ladies to finish their meals and shot straight off home. At last I knew the way forward. Better to know what was going on than continue a life of worry and uncertainty. As I headed down the street, my head was full of calm and soothing thoughts, interrupted only by Mrs Norton's plaintive cry, 'When shall we three eat meat again?'

30 Friday

Stephen's out in his cab taking a fare to an address a couple of streets away, so I should have a few hours to carry out my little plan. I suddenly feel a little sick. What will I find? Oh well, here goes nothing . . .

Oh well. There *went* nothing. I should have known the shed would be locked. I didn't expect it to be electrified and surrounded by infra-red beams, though. Whatever Stephen's got in there, he clearly doesn't want me to find out. Or, by the looks of it, the SAS, MI5 or the CIA.

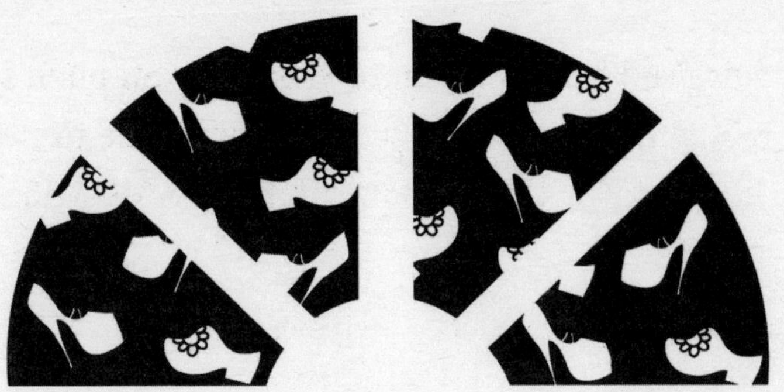

October

1 Saturday

Stephen's just got back from the Red Lion and he doesn't look at all well, even by his standards. I asked him what was the matter but he just slumped on the sofa without saying a word, staring at the flying ducks. After well over an hour I finally managed to get it out of him. Apparently, the pub's got a new landlord. Stephen doesn't cope very well with change.

2 Sunday

Oh dear. Stephen's just back from the pub and he looks even worse than yesterday. This time it took all my powers of persuasion, and a four-pack of Stella, to get it out of him. It turns out that not only has the Red Lion got a new landlord – it's getting a complete makeover. Stephen doesn't know all the details but there's talk of ferns and bookshelves and flatbread wraps. Actually, I have to say it sounds rather nice.

3 Monday

Stephen's spent all day on the phone to the brewery to find out exactly what's happening to his beloved Red Lion. It would appear that it's going to be the flagship for the brewery's 'foray into the young professional market' and 'spearhead a new economically relevant chain of continental-style socio-alcoholic environments'. Apparently, it's going to be completely redecorated and renamed 'Le Lion Rouge'. Poor Stephen. He doesn't know what to do with himself. He just keeps rocking back and forth in the foetal position, sobbing and mumbling, 'Gastropub . . . gastropub . . .'

4 Tuesday

Just had a phone call from the pub. It sounds like Stephen found out what to do with himself. I'd better get over there straight away . . .

Deary me! Whatever is that husband of mine like? As soon as I'd finished watching *Murder She Thought* and drunk my second cup of tea, I set off for the Red Lion. The landlord ushered me directly to the gents' toilets, where Stephen had chained himself to the urinals. Apparently, they're due to be demolished on Thursday to make way for a modern unisex arrangement, and Stephen finally cracked when he heard the news. Of course, I did all any wife could do. I told him not to be such a pillock, and went home.

5 Wednesday

Now, that's more like it! Finally, this poetry course is coming to life. Ms Wordsmith has obviously recognised that the rest of the group are holding a true poet like myself back from really nailing my muse. The subject of this evening's session was Existential Verse. At last, a proper opportunity to show those literary wannabes what real poetry's all about. While exploring the deepest, darkest recesses of my soul, of course.

Inevitably, the others floundered. It should be interesting to hear their attempts next week. Meanwhile, all I have to do is follow Ms Wordsmith's instructions to 'reach into the soulless abyss and touch the futility and despair of human existence'. I told her I would get straight to it, just as soon as I'd been to visit Stephen in the pub toilets, cooked the kids their dinner and watched *Diagnosis Natural Causes* over a slice of Battenberg. She said that was exactly the kind of thing I should be going for. I always knew I was a natural.

6 Thursday

D-day. Or possibly bidet, if the brewery gets its way. The demolition of the Red Lion toilets is due to begin at noon so there's no time to lose . . . I'm heading down there now to see if Stephen's come to his senses.

Goodness, Diary, what a traumatic day! I arrived only just in time (I had the dry cleaning to pick up, and Mrs Norton's coffee mornings do drag on so). Stephen looked terrible. Tired, drawn and clearly in need of a meal.

From the other side of the toilet wall, I could hear the low rumble of a bulldozer. Without stopping to think, I reached inside my hatband and drew out a small key. Weak from lack of lager, Stephen only put up minimal resistance as I unlocked one of the cuffs. I took a deep breath as I heard the rumble increase steadily but it was too late. I had already done it! Stephen smiled wearily at me and I smiled back. If he was going to go then so was I.

I placed the empty cuff around my wrist and locked it. As I kneeled before the porcelain, I braced myself . . .

Suddenly, there was a loud roar, and I saw my life flush before my eyes . . .

7 Friday

I'm sorry, Diary. I was shaking too much to write any more last night after the traumatic events at the Red Lion. Stephen and I were only inches from death when the urinal's automatic flush doused us both. Luckily, the shock of the sudden shower brought me to my senses and in an instant I'd unlocked the handcuffs and dragged Stephen to the safety of a cubicle. No sooner had the sign clicked to 'engaged' than we heard a thunderous crash of steel, brick and porcelain and the urinals were no more.

8 Saturday

First Saturday morning lie-in with Stephen for ages. Unfortunately, it was because TakeU4ARide Cabs have chosen to dispense with his services. They cited a number of reasons – poor customer relations, no sense of direction, complete disregard for the Highway Code and failure to turn up for work for three days as a result of being chained to a public urinal. Thank goodness Stephen has an alternative career to fall back on. I'll fetch his ladder and bucket . . .

9 Sunday

For a special treat, we took the kids to the snow dome this afternoon. They just love it when it's turned over and all the pretty snowflakes float down on top of the plastic Tower Bridge.

10 Monday

The kids are at school and Stephen's out on his window-cleaning round so at last a bit of peace and quiet for me to write my poem for Wednesday's class. I'll try some ideas out on you, Diary, before writing the final version on my best notepaper.

But first, a cup of tea. Just to give the brain cells a bit of a boost.

Time for a second cup of tea. Then I'll really be ready to get started.

Just one more cup, I think. To get me firing on all creative cylinders.

Maybe it's too peaceful and quiet. I'm clearly not used to it. Perhaps I'll just pop the radio on for a little background noise to help me focus properly. I'll try that new station. Ooh lovely, Bryan Adams . . .

I must say, listening to Infinity Number One FM is really helping. They only play singles that topped the charts for at least two months, which is a sure sign of quality and means every one of the half-dozen records on their playlist is a classic. Whitney Houston, for example, is the perfect accompaniment to a Cup-a-Soup, no matter how many times you hear her.

Hooray! Out of absolutely nowhere, inspiration has struck. I knew my plan would work. I've finally got a title. In fact, I have two. Goodness knows where they came from. Now I just need to choose which one to use – 'I Will Always Love Soup' or 'Everything I Brew, I Brew It For You'.

11 Tuesday

Stephen should be on his window-cleaning round right now but he's forgotten his bucket. And his ladder. And to get out of bed.

12 Wednesday

Poetry class tonight and the world premiere of my existential masterpiece! And all my classmates' poems, too. I have to admit to feeling ever so slightly nervous when it finally came to my turn. After all, I had invested a great deal of time, soul-searching and tea in my creation. But, ever the professional – in approach, if not remuneration – I put my fears aside, stood proudly up, cleared my throat and began . . .

'Bohemian Spam For Tea' by Edna Fry (Mrs)

Am I his real wife?
Is this just fantasy?
I've bought up the large size,
No escaping there's Spam for tea.

Open your eyes,
Look at Stephen Fry and see
He's not a poor boy,
He needs no sympathy
Because he's easy come, easyJet,
Littlewoods, little bet,
When he's cleaning windows,

Nothing really matters to Steve
To Steve . . .
Stephen,
Just gone to shop,
Put my coin into the slot,
Took my trolley, off I trot.
Stephen,
I am almost done,
(Better leave before my husband hits the roof . . .)
Stephen,
(Oo-oo-oo . . . any way the wheels go . . .)
Didn't mean to make you wait,
If I'm not back by ten, just watch a movie . . .
Carry On, Carry On . . . Doctor, Nurse or Up the Khyber

Midnight,
That time has come.
Got jelly down my thigh,
Strawberry mivvi in my eye.
Lie back, think of England, this can't go on,
Gotta leek in my behind that faces south.
Stephen . . .

(Oo-oo-oo – did we close the windows?)
You used to be so shy,
I sometimes wish you'd never watched porn at all . . .
I see a little pink stiletto in the van,
Sharon Hughes, Sharon Hughes, did you do the hand tango?
Underpants and night things really quite enlightening me.

Gallivanting, gallivanting,
Gallivanting, puff 'n' panting,
Gallivanting, there she blows.
Fellatio-oh-oh-oh!

I'm just a poor wife,
Nobody loves me.
(She's just a poor wife from a poor family
Spare her some time and a nice cup of tea.)

He's an ape. He's a beast. Should've been a
priest . . .

Gorilla? Me? I'm waiting for my tea!
Let me be!

Gorilla? Me? I'm waiting for my tea!
Let me be!
Gorilla? Still waiting for my tea!
Let me see!
I'm going down the pub!
Watch TV!
Then maybe to a club!
Oh please don't go oh-oh-oh!
Ho! Ho! Ho! Ho! Ho! Ho! Ho!

Sitting here, with a beer and Mamma Mia video!
He's down the pub and there's devilled eggs and Spam
For tea
For tea
For tea . . . !

So you think you can treat me like some kind of
slave?
And I don't mean the times when we just misbehave!
Oh Stephen!
Just want something more even!

(Just gonna drink stout. Looks like we're all right out of beer . . .)

Ooh yeah, ooh yeah . . .

Nothing really matters,
Easy to believe,
Nothing really matters,
'cept beer and birds and ladders
To Steve . . .

(When he's cleaning windows . . .)

I think it's safe to say I made quite an impact.

13 Thursday

I can't believe it! The *Daily Herald*'s running a poetry competition! What perfect timing, given the reception my poem received at the class last night. It clearly deserves to be read by a wider audience. Why should all those thousands of people miss out on the opportunity to read a work of pure genius and originality like 'Bohemian Spam For Tea'? I'll send it off this morning! Fame beckons . . .

14 Friday

Received a very prompt telephone call from the editor of the *Daily Herald* this morning. She said that although my entry had a great deal of merit, regrettably they were unable to consider it for inclusion in their poetry competition due to its 'evident plagiaristic nature'. I told her I had no idea what she was talking about and she said something about the Queen and mercury. Poor woman's clearly been spending too much time around the printing ink. I was about to slam down the receiver in disgust when she asked if, instead, the newspaper might possibly interview me about my life with 'the great Stephen Fry'. She said her readers might find my story highly entertaining. I said I had no idea what was so great about Stephen nor whether my 'story' would be in any way entertaining, but I would be only too happy to oblige, so she told me to expect a reporter on Monday morning. What a strange woman.

15 Saturday

Stephen's sleepwalking again. It's amazing – every night he manages to find his way to the pub just before last orders.

16 Sunday

Honestly, I told Stephen not to eat Spanish food in the bath. Now he's got his toe stuck in the tapas.

17 Monday

What a fascinating afternoon. The reporter from the *Daily Herald* turned up just after noon.

Apparently, he'd been delayed by the protracted birth of the local zoo's first albino polar bear cub. He was a very well-dressed young man, clearly terribly intelligent. He complimented me on my home and my custard creams. We chatted for hours – or rather I did, while he scribbled away in his little notebook. He asked all sorts of questions, mostly about Stephen, although I managed to redirect him to the subject of my literary prowess most of the time. He smiled and nodded attentively at every answer and before I knew it, it was six o'clock and he had to go. He told me the article would be appearing in Wednesday's edition. It was sure to make quite a splash, he said.

18 Tuesday

Poor Stephen. Ever since the Red Lion closed for renovations he's been forced to venture further and further afield to satisfy his karaoke habit. Tonight he's at the Ballad 'n' Blues Burger Bar on the high street.

19 Wednesday

Couldn't sleep last night. I was far too excited. As soon as Stephen had gone off on his round and I'd given the kids their Alcopoptarts, I dashed straight round to the newsagent to pick up today's *Daily Herald*. To my astonishment, they said they had sold out. Already! I checked my watch, disbelievingly. It was still only five past nine. That reporter must have been right. I clearly had made a splash! I hurried to the 24-hour garage but it was the same story there. Goodness. I had no idea I was so popular. Well, I had an inkling, obviously, but I'm far too modest to admit it.

After scouring the entire district, I was reluctantly forced to return home empty-handed. I was out so long I even missed tonight's poetry class, ironically. Or is it metaphysically? Anyway, in the end, I tried ringing the offices of the *Herald* but even they didn't have any copies left. They'd never known anything like it. Not even when Princess Michael of Kent opened the new Matalan.

20 Thursday

I knew I shouldn't have offered to help Brangelina make that giant butterfly costume for school assembly. Me and my big moth.

21 Friday

An interesting morning, to say the least. I was busy doing a spot of cleaning when I noticed something sticking out from under Stephen's side of the bed. At first I assumed it was just another copy of *East Anglian Babes*, but when I looked closer I had quite a shock. It was a copy of the *Daily Herald*. Wednesday's *Daily Herald*. And there on the front cover, next to a rather fetching photograph of myself holding a teapot, in bold black letters, were the words: 'STEPHEN FRY'S SECRET WIFE LIFTS THE LID!'

I sat down heavily on the bed. Very heavily. The mattress seemed much harder than usual. I looked underneath and couldn't believe what

I saw. Lying there were what looked like hundreds of copies of the *Herald* – each bearing the same headline. He must have bought the lot! This could only mean one thing. He must love me even more than I realised!

22 Saturday

Usual Saturday night in. Stephen's at Sing-along-a-sushi. I hope the Red Lion opens again soon.

23 Sunday

Still no idea who the father of Viennetta's child is. We've narrowed it down to three, we think – it's either Darren, an assistant tattoo artist; Gavin, a shelf-stacker at Foodland; or Raymond, a one-legged Dutchman. We're hoping it's Raymond. He's got a PhD in Physics, the clever clog.

24 Monday

Wonder what's happened to Hugh Junior this evening? He's not generally this late home from school. I hope he hasn't wandered off again with his imaginary friend, Hugh Junior Junior.

25 Tuesday

Finally found Hugh Junior late last night, sitting in the local woods with a torch and a pile of Stephen's *Razzle* magazines. No wonder he was in a spinney. An educational night all round. Hugh Junior discovered that Britnee from Newport likes broad shoulders and Curly Wurlys and I found exactly who – or what – Hugh Junior Junior is. And why he enjoys playing with him quite so much.

26 Wednesday

Apologised to Ms Wordsmith for not attending last week's class. She said it hadn't been the same without me. What a nice lady. Today we tried our hand at rhyming couplets. I managed several – Wayne and Jane, Andy and Mandy, and Belinda and Gurinder (although strictly speaking, I think that last one's a mixed metaphor).

27 Thursday

Oh dear. Brangelina's nightmares have started again. She keeps going on about this man who's been invading her dreams. According to her, he always looks exactly the same. He wears a long striped jumper and a hat and he can be absolutely anywhere – standing behind a tree, lurking in an alleyway, even hiding behind her wardrobe. I do wish Stephen wouldn't read her *Where's Wally?* at bedtime.

28 Friday

Today is the grand opening, or re-opening, of Le Lion Rouge. I think it's very much to Stephen's credit that he's prepared to set aside his prejudices and pay the establishment a brief visit. I told him he was doing a fine thing as it could only be good for the *entente cordiale*, but Stephen insists he'll be sticking to lager.

29 Saturday

No sign of Stephen since last night's text, which simply consisted of those three little words that say so little and yet so much – meklili skaloo phadunk. But that's Stephen. After half a dozen pints, he's completely unpredictable.

30 Sunday

Still no sign of Stephen, although by all accounts a man answering his description was seen in the Botanical Gardens singing 'La Marseillaise' to a giant fern.

31 Monday

Hallowe'en – the night *he* came home. Just in time too. Mrs Winton's party began at eight. It had a mythological theme – I, of course, made a sensational Aphrodite, while Stephen was some kind of half-man, half-beast. At least, until he changed into his costume. The highlight of the evening was when Mrs Norton and Mrs Biggins both turned up as Medusa. If looks could kill . . .

November

1 Tuesday

Struggling to get Stephen out of bed this morning. He says he's not feeling well, poor dear. I'll try looking up his symptoms on Hypochondria.com. I hope it's nothing too serious – it's bingo night.

2 Wednesday

How disappointing. I received a letter this morning from the council insisting I give up my little Ednables venture – apparently the school was objecting on the grounds that I was providing unfair competition with my 'blatantly commercial approach'. Really! It's hardly my fault if they don't give out loyalty cards and small plastic toys with their meals! It's the children I feel sorry for. How are they supposed to complete their Ednimals collection now?

Stephen's complaining that he's feeling even worse today. His temperature's 98.6 degrees and his blood pressure is 120 over 80. There's no doubt about it – he's got man 'flu. Looks like I'll have to miss my poetry class and do my Florence Nightingale impression. Just as well I kept the cap and lamp from our 'Kinky Crimea' night.

3 Thursday

Oh dear. It looks like poor Stephen's worse than I thought. According to the chemist, it sounds like he may have the Common Cold. Obviously, I said I knew there was nothing that could cure that but she directed my attention to a small fluorescent packet on a brightly coloured display stand near the counter. She said Stemsip was still in the experimental stage but that the company developing it was highly ethical and didn't believe in testing its products on animals, hence it was on sale to the general public for a limited period of time.

I took a packet from the stand and examined the back:

1 sachet to be taken, dissolved in water, every four hours, three days or whenever required.

Warning: May cause drowsiness, blurred vision, inflamed larynx, sneezing fits, dizziness, dyslexia, irrational bursts of aggression and premature death.

It seemed all right. No different from an average night down the pub for Stephen.

4 Friday

Oh, deary me. I've given Stephen three doses so far and, if anything, he seems worse. The stutter and hair loss are certainly new. Looks like I'll have to tell him to miss Le Lion Rouge's first karaoke night. And he had 'Joe le Taxi' word perfect too, poor dear . . .

How remarkable! No sooner had the word karaoke passed my lips than Stephen made a full recovery. Those sachets must be better than I thought. I must write a letter to Cold Comfort Pharmaceuticals and thank them!

5 Saturday

Bonfire night. Such a pity that living in this area means we have to tape our letterbox closed at this time of year, but if we don't, the neighbours will only go and complain when the kids shoot rockets out at them.

6 Sunday

I was doing a spot of essential cleaning this morning – the teapot, the teacups, the teaspoons – when I came across a folded piece of paper. I opened it up and was startled to see it was the 'F' page from our National Treasure Trust handbook! Goodness only knows how it got inside the smoothie-maker – just as well I never use it. I was even more surprised when I examined it closer to find it contained not only Forsyth Towers but a certain Fry Hall!

Of course, I immediately showed it to Stephen and suggested we have a family trip there this afternoon. He seemed slightly reluctant until I pointed out that he might be related to the owners, then he seemed very reluctant. Honestly, I'll never understand that man as long as I live.

Anyway, after much arm twisting and several Chinese burns we finally all piled into the car and were on our way. I have to say, it was a much longer journey than I had anticipated, what with all the winding lanes, dirt tracks and ferry crossings and it was dark by the time we finally arrived. Frustratingly, it had just closed to visitors for the day so Stephen was forced to turn the car round and drive us straight back home again. Funny how the mind plays tricks on you. It seemed a much shorter – and straighter – journey home. Oh well, as I said to Stephen, we'll just have to try again next week.

7 Monday

Bin day. It takes the whole day for the lorry to get round to our street, what with all the different bins we have now – there's the one for paper, the one for plastics, the one for garden waste and the big one for recycle bin instructional leaflets.

8 Tuesday

That's the last time I let Stephen watch *Star Trek*. He's refusing to go out to work in case his actions affect the future. Considering the rate he works I should think that's highly unlikely.

9 Wednesday

Poetry class this evening. I must say, I think I've really discovered my 'voice'. When I finally found the new room (they moved when I was away last week and neglected to tell me, the scamps) I wowed everyone with my two new masterpieces, 'Under Milk Stout' and 'The Rum of the Ancient Mariner'.

10 Thursday

One of my favourite days of the year – Christmas baking day. I've decided against making my usual Twelve Days of Christmas Pudding this year – it's getting harder and harder to find good pipers – so instead I'm trying my own variation on the recipe in Delia's *Come On, Let's Be Having Yule.* I only hope Tesco haven't run out of tuna and hundreds and thousands.

11 Friday

A bitterly cold day. Stephen managed to get himself stuck to the lamp-post again. At least it was only his tongue this time.

12 Saturday

Finally got our suitcase back from the airline after our holiday – I'd completely forgotten they'd lost it. Just as well, as Stephen was running out of underpants and the baby was starting to get a bit claustrophobic.

13 Sunday

Right, the sandwiches are packed, the flasks are filled with tea and the twins are safely secured to the roof rack – Fry Hall, here we come . . .

After an almost continual two hours of 'Are we nearly there yet?' and my repeated replies, 'You should know, dear, you're driving,' we finally drew up at the gates of an imposing, ivy-covered building. My feet tingled with excitement as we drove up the long gravel path and saw, etched into the masonry above the tall oak door – Hunniford House.

Stephen shrugged his shoulders, grinned apologetically and pointed at the sat nav. I sighed. Since we were there, we may as well have a look round, I thought.

In actual fact, Hunniford House was rather nice, with its gables and gift shop, and we spent a fascinating hour or so there but I was all too eager to get on the road again so that we might make it to Fry Hall before nightfall this time.

After 40 minutes we stopped again. This time we were parked in front of a sixteenth-century moat house. I checked the sign. Noakes Cottage. I looked at Stephen. Again he pointed to the sat nav.

All in all, we visited 12 Treasure Trust properties today, not one of them Fry Hall. From the Katona Pondlife Centre in Bude to Lorraine Kelly Castle in Auchtermuchtie, defeated and despondent, we returned home. It's almost as if that sat nav doesn't want us to go there – or someone doesn't.

14 Monday

Received an email from Mr deClarkson this morning detailing his latest amendments to the school timetable. On the face of it, it all looks terribly exciting and no doubt has its educational value, but I can't help wondering about the new phonic approach to Home Economics and what appears to be an over-reliance on balloon animals in the History curriculum.

15 Tuesday

Ah, that distinctive musty autumn scent. So evocative. Then all too soon it's over and Stephen's changed into his winter pants.

16 Wednesday

A slightly upsetting evening at poetry class tonight. Angela (a little informal, I know, but she insisted I call her that – apparently, no one else in the group calls her Ms Wordsmith) gave me my termly review. She said my work was 'derivative, unimaginative and aesthetically redundant'. If that's what she thinks of me I can only imagine what she makes of the rest of the class!

17 Thursday

Autumn term parents' evening tonight. As part of Mr deClarkson's new, forward-thinking educational regime, it was presented through the medium of shadow theatre, each teacher visible only in silhouette behind a paper screen. Despite the new approach, it was still the same standard feedback – only this time the teachers didn't need to force a smile when they greeted us – but the good news is that Brangelina has been put forward for the school gymnastics team, being the only pupil capable of a full backward somersault with side twist and 360-degree cranial rotation.

18 Friday

After Wednesday's poetry class, I thought I might try something different next term. I've been thinking about doing the Life Painting course, but there's something I'm not comfortable about and that's the bottom line.

19 Saturday

I've cooked roast lamb for lunch today. It looks and smells delicious, even if I do say so myself. A shame we're out of mint sauce, but we've got plenty of Listerine.

20 Sunday

At last – Fry Hall! After all this time, I can't believe it! The journey took a while – largely because every few miles Stephen had to stop and get out of the car to make 'a very important phone call' – no doubt regarding the very important matter of the 3.30 at Kempton. Anyway, we got there in the end and I have to say it was well worth the wait! The grounds alone were worth the visit, from the Quite Interesting Gardens to the 'Goodness, What Larks!' adventure park complete with monkey bars and the thrilling 'Mr Fry's Wilde Ride'. And when we finally entered the house, what a vision of opulence greeted our eyes – from the 120-seat silver dining table to the magnificent emerald chandeliers in the Wagner room and even the Elizabethan-style café with its pitchers of Dorian Gray tea and Melchett in Your Mouth chocolate muffins. I was overwhelmed. There was even a giant shield above the fireplace bearing the Fry family crest and motto – 'Moab . . . ' something or other – I assume it was Latin. The only disappointment was all the drapes. Apparently, every one of the family portraits was being restored that weekend and so they were covered from the public during the process.

Now, Diary, you know I've never been one to

flout rules but I have to admit that my curiosity did get the better of me. Who could blame me? After all, this place could give us a big clue as to Stephen's ancestry – and who knows what else? I waited until the security guard was distracted by a child sliding down the banister of the Great Staircase (no idea who it was. Either Asbo or Subo) and sidled up to a particularly grand looking gilt-framed painting at the foot of the stairs. I looked round and when I was quite sure no one was watching me, I reached out and pulled up a corner of the cloth that hung over the picture. All I could make out was a foot and the artist's signature – a Mr Harris, it looked like – so I raised the material further until eventually light fell on the subject's face.

I stifled a small squeal as I stared on those features. Whoever it was standing there on that heath, surrounded by stags and shotguns, was the spitting image of my Stephen! My head in a spin, I raced to the next picture and looked at that. There it was again – Stephen's unmistakeable face beaming out at me from the canvas. I tried another. And another.

Whether a gentleman in his finery, a young boy at his mother's breast or an old lady screaming on a bridge, each bore the inimitable face of my husband!

Before I had time to tell Stephen, I was suddenly startled by the wail of an alarm, a deep voice booming out 'Intruder alert!' over the tannoy system and a dozen security guards charging into the room. Instinctively, I pushed through a door marked private and turned the key on the inside.

Breathing heavily, I tried to collect my thoughts as fists pounded on the door. My eyes darted round. I seemed to be in some kind of study. Sitting on a huge, leather-topped desk, a computer hummed quietly. I made my way round the desk and sat in a big chair to see a white screen covered in type and a cursor blinking expectantly. I had just screwed up my eyes to make out what was written when I was aware of a shuffling sound behind me.

I turned in time to see the long curtain beside the French window twitch very slightly. I looked to the floor and there, peeking out from under the hem, were the tips of two training shoes. I coughed and they sharply withdrew under the material. Taking a deep breath, I stood up silently and reached forward.

The tannoy suddenly crackled to life again.

'Pay no attention to that man behind the curtain!' it boomed.

Time slowed to a crawl as I watched my fingers close round the edge of the curtain.

'Do as I say!' roared the deep voice. 'The great and powerful Fry has spoken!'

I pulled back the curtain. Standing there, with a microphone in his hand and an open mouth was . . . Stephen!

My mind whirled, my legs felt weak and suddenly everything was black . . .

When I eventually woke, I was home. In my own bed. And Stephen and the kids were standing over me with concerned looks on their faces.

'But . . . what? Oh, Stephen,' I mumbled. 'I'm back.'

He looked across at the children and patted my hand gently.

'But I've been away. In a wonderful place. And you were there . . . and you . . . and you. And you . . .'

They all laughed.

I sighed. I couldn't believe it had been a dream – it all seemed so real. But I guess it's true what they say. There's no place like a stately home.

21 Monday

Oh dear. I'm sorry, Diary. I'm sure I have no idea what happened to me yesterday. At least I got a nice long sleep – my first in ages, what with all the worry about Stephen. And Brangelina. And Stephen Junior. All of them, to be honest. At least I feel better now. I think I'll take a nice relaxing stroll into town to get a bit of fresh air. Well, air . . .

Had a lovely walk. I must say, on a sunny morning, it's actually not such a bad place. It's just a shame about the litter, and the graffiti –

and the overriding smell of urine. Oh, and all the fly-posters everywhere, covering up perfectly good walls and sides of buses – for a minute I even thought I saw Stephen's face on the number 68, but before I had the chance to take a proper look, the lights had changed and it was gone.

22 Tuesday

After last week's assessment, I was determined to write something truly exceptional for this week's poem, but I just couldn't concentrate with Stephen droning away in the background. I asked him to stop but it made no difference. He just kept going on, demanding my undivided attention. But the most worrying thing is, when I finally gave up and looked round, the sofa was empty. And yet there he was, still talking. I was beginning to think I might be going mad, when I realised it was just the radio! For some reason, it seemed to be tuned to Radio 4 – can't imagine why. They very rarely play any thrash metal. I turned it off and the room fell silent. What a relief. And yet, it did sound an *awful* lot like Stephen . . .

23 Wednesday

Missed poetry class this evening. After the business with the radio yesterday I just couldn't settle to writing, so I put the television on, and whose face was grinning out at me in widescreen? Stephen's! I grabbed the remote and turned over. There he was again. I flicked through the channels. Again his face. Again. And again. I grabbed my coat, shot out of the house and jumped straight on the bus to the medical centre, pretending to ignore his face on the side of it.

Doctor Tarantino was terribly nice. And awfully understanding. I told him about seeing my husband's face everywhere I go and he said that I was obviously under a great deal of stress at the moment. He said there was only one cure he could recommend. I needed some time to relax, preferably away from the rest of the family. Ha! Chance would be a fine thing! I suppose I do still have that money from the *Daily Herald* but there's no way Stephen would ever let me go away, I'm quite sure of that. He can barely cope when I have a long bath.

24 Thursday

Told Stephen what the doctor said yesterday and was amazed by his response. He said he agreed completely and that he'd be only too happy to look after the children while I had a nice relaxing weekend away. He even said he'd find me the perfect place and book it for me himself if I just gave him my credit card details. He seemed genuinely caring and supportive. Now I know I need a break!

After an hour's Googling, Stephen proudly announced that he'd found the perfect place for me to unwind. A health spa just a few miles away. He's booked me in for tomorrow for their special 'Mmm' weekend.

25 Friday

Goodness, I'm tired. Spent all night preparing meals for Stephen and the kids for while I'm away. I wouldn't have been able to relax until I knew the fridge was fully stocked with all the delicacies they're used to. I just hope they can cope without all the other things I provide – the warmth, the love and the over 80 per cent name-recall rate.

Stephen dropped me off at the health spa after tea. I must say the place looks lovely. All gleaming and white, just like a huge wedding cake but without the bride and groom on the top. Well, without the groom. And to be honest, the bride wasn't there all that long either.
I must say, it was quite a shock to see the spa manageress hanging from that gargoyle by her wedding train, although her successor reassured me that it was just a tragic accident

– she had merely been trying on her dress in advance of her impending marriage when the picture on her television had deteriorated and she had quite naturally climbed onto the roof to adjust the aerial – and most certainly not foul play of any kind.

My room was terribly nice. No doubt it had been designed to be calming. The decor was light and simple, the bed firm but comfortable. And the Valium tablet on the pillow was a lovely touch.

26 Saturday

Woke up feeling refreshed and full of energy. I thought I'd find it difficult to get to sleep without Stephen in the bed but it actually proved a great deal easier than with him next to me.

After a light breakfast of llama yoghurt and assorted berries, I examined the brochure to see which treatment to choose first. I opted for the reflexology, although I have to say I was a little disappointed. The therapist just kept hitting my knee with a small hammer.

I had been hoping for an aromatherapy treatment after lunch but apparently the therapist had unexpectedly passed away from exhaustion during the night. According to the new manager she'd been burning the candle at both ends.

Instead, I plucked up my courage and decided to try an enema – Mrs Winton's been raving about them for years. They had a variety of different options – water, even coffee. Of course I chose the English Breakfast tea. I have to say, it was an eye-watering experience, but it was all right in the end. Although it might have benefited from a HobNob.

27 Sunday

Was awakened in the early morning to the sound of screams. When I went to investigate I was informed that one of the guests had unfortunately passed away. Apparently, he was having one of their festive treatments, the Santa Special – Beard, Sack and Crack – when he reacted badly to the wax they were using. The new manageress said it was a simple accident. They'd made a list of guests with life-threatening allergies but they hadn't checked it twice. It certainly wasn't foul play of any kind, she insisted.

After breakfast, I checked the brochure again. I was tempted by the wildebeest semen hair treatment, but I do so hate to remove my hat in public so I just went for a quick brim bleach instead. Unfortunately, there were only sandwiches for lunch as the chef had unexpectedly drowned in his own jojoba and coriander soup.

I decided to spend the afternoon in my room. It seemed the safest option. Besides, the chalk outlines around the hall weren't particularly conducive to relaxation.

28 Monday

Not a very restful night. I was woken at midnight by a blood-curdling scream, at one by a gunshot and at two by a series of explosions. At breakfast, I spilt most of my hypoallergenic cereal due to my hand shaking and could barely sign my own name as I checked out.

I was practically in tears as the receptionist thanked me for my stay and asked if I'd manage to solve it. I asked her what she meant and she said that was the whole point of the triple M weekend. Triple M? Didn't she mean 'Mmm', I said? She frowned and handed me a leaflet. I stared down at the small piece of paper fluttering in my fingers and read it. Typical! Trust Stephen to book me into a Murder, Mystery & Mayhem weekend.

29 Tuesday

Funnily enough, despite everything, I think that weekend away has actually done me a lot of good. I haven't seen Stephen's face anywhere other than where it should be and I feel calm, relaxed and perfectly sane. In fact, I feel so good I think I'll write a poem. After all, the sun is singing, the clouds are shining and there's not a bird in the sky.

30 Wednesday

Went to poetry class. I read my poem, 'All Work and No Play Makes Edna a Dull Girl'. Ms Wordsmith seemed suitably impressed, noting the 'particularly effective use of repetition throughout the entire 37 pages'. In fact, she said it was so powerful and evocative that it would be a good idea, for a change of pace, to listen to a completely different reading, and she took a CD from her bag. She placed it in the player on her desk and sat back with her eyes closed, instructing us to do the same so that the words may 'wash over us and cleanse us'.

I shut my eyes and waited. And then came the voice: cool, precise and mellifluous – and Stephen's. I opened my eyes, stood up and left the room.

Now I see what it is I have to do. There's no question about it. I have no choice.

December

1 Thursday

Dear Diary, I'm so sorry I couldn't tell you about my plans yesterday. I couldn't risk you falling into the wrong hands. I knew it would take military precision for my plan to work so I synchronised my watch and waited . . .

08:25 Children leave house and turn left down street in direction of school before carrying out 180-degree turn and heading to Brian's Bowl-a-rama.

09:15 Stephen leaves house to go out on window-cleaning round. Heads in direction of her at number 38. Estimated time of return 12:00 to 16:00 hours, depending on level of blue pill intake.

09:23 Leave house in best hat, carrying one large holdall, empty.

10:46 Return to house carrying one large holdall containing saw, industrial strength bolt-cutter, flame-thrower, gelignite and book, *A Bluffer's Guide to Breaking and Entering.*

11:15 Go back to Argos to get best hat.

11:28 Return to house. Employ reasonable force to gain entry to Stephen's shed.

11:52 Employ unreasonable force to gain entry to Stephen's shed.

11:53 Place remains of shed door in appropriate bin.

11:58 Enter shed.

I stepped into what was left of Stephen's shed and looked around. I couldn't believe what I was seeing. There, through the slowly clearing smoke, sitting on a small leather-topped desk was a computer, just like the one I had dreamt about in Fry Hall. And beside it were reams and reams of bound and severely charred sheets of typewritten pages. And not a can of beer or copy of *Humungous Hooters* to be seen.

I brushed the cinders from the chair and my hair and sat down heavily. So, all the time he was in his shed, Stephen wasn't attempting to brew the perfect lager, after all. But then what? Had he been writing something all this time? How could this be? What with his aversion to literature and to adjectives in particular. It didn't make any sense.

And then it struck me – as the shed wall collapsed. A bookshelf. I stared down at the floor. There they all were, lying at my feet – *Roget's Thesaurus, The Complete Works of Oscar Wilde, A Guide to the Poolside Flora and Fauna of Stelios* . . . And as I rubbed my head, it slowly started to fall into place – the long hours spent in this shed and on the road, the Blackpool débâcle, the newspapers under the bed, Fry Hall, Stephen's face and voice everywhere I went . . .

So what now? I stared at the computer, the books, the sheets of paper and the smouldering remains of the shed and I knew I had no choice. I had to confront him. To find out what all this was about. To find out just who my husband really was.

12:09 Stephen returns home to get more blue pills.

12:10 Explain to Stephen about gas leak.

2 Friday

Oh dear, Diary. I wish I knew what to do. I feel as if I've been living a lie all these years. Or rather, Stephen has. At least now I know I wasn't going mad. Maybe it would have been better if I was. At least I wouldn't be feeling so lost and empty. Or maybe I would, but with a potato up my nose. I think I'll just go back to bed. I doubt anyone will notice.

3 Saturday

I was right. No one noticed. Still couldn't face getting out of bed this morning. There didn't seem any point. Brangelina came up at one point to see how I was and to ask could she please have a raise in her pocket money? Stephen seems to be avoiding me. He hasn't said any more about the shed – or what's left of it. Neither have I. I just don't know what to say. I can't even bring myself to read the sheet of paper I pocketed from the shed. I may as well tear it up and throw it on the floor.

I was about to turn over and try to get back to sleep for the eighth time when I heard a strange noise drifting through the window. At first I assumed it was just another car alarm but then I realised it was more melodic. Well, slightly more melodic. I reached across and opened the window to see a small group of hooded youths standing on the doorstep with their hands in their pockets, swaying back and forth. I watched them blearily for a little while before eventually I realised what they were. At once, I felt my heart lift and a broad smile cross my face. Carol singers!

I leaned out of the window and shouted down.

'You, boy, what's today?'

The tallest of the three frowned and looked at his digital watch.

'Today?' he cried. 'Why, it's the third of December.'

'Oh, good!' I shouted back. 'Then I haven't missed it. Now why don't you all toddle off and come back nearer Christmas Day. And get a bit more practice in while you're at it.'

I shut the window and jumped out of bed with a huge smile on my face. A Christmas miracle!

4 Sunday

I do love this time of year! There's nothing quite like Christmas to help you push your worries to one side and focus on a whole new load. There's the cards to write, the presents to buy and the Spam to baste. So much to do! I'll start with brushing these pieces of paper under the carpet.

5 Monday

Before I do anything else, I'd better write the traditional Fry round-robin Christmas letter. I know how desperate everyone must be to know what we've been up to this year.

Dear All,

A very warm and yuletidy festive period to you all. We in the Fry household hope this finds you hale and hearty. I have so much to tell you, dears. Goodness, what a year it has been!

To begin with, the biggest news is that Stephen and I are soon to be grandparents. I can imagine what you're thinking – how is that possible, at our tender ages? – but it's true! Our very own little Viennetta isn't quite so little at the moment. In just a few weeks she'll be giving birth to a bouncing baby boy. Or girl. Or twins. We're not sure – the scan wasn't entirely conclusive. Of course, she and her husband-to-be, Blaine (a brain surgeon and part-time pilot from Boston in America), are as over the moon as we are and have already put him/her/them down for Yale.

Stephen Junior has started drama school and has already been marked out as a star of the future. According to his acting coach, he possesses the brooding intensity of a young Brando combined with the comic timing of Chaplin and hell-raising potential of Rourke. Of course, we wouldn't want to second guess the Academy but Stephen's putting up a shelf big enough to fit the odd little gold man, just in case.

Hugh Junior, I'm afraid to say, is our only disappointment. He just sits in his room all day doing his homework and playing with his chemistry set – hardly proper behaviour for a young teenage boy. If it wasn't for the excessive bouts of self-abuse, we'd be really quite concerned.

Brangelina continues to astound her teacher, currently excelling in the areas of alternative religion, and the twins are a year older and beginning to develop their own, highly distinctive personalities – in fact, they're so individual, sometimes I struggle to tell they're twins.

As for Stephen and I, we're still the very epitome of love's young dream, walking hand in hand down life's rose-tinted highway. We shared a beautiful weekend in Paris – more like a second honeymoon, really – had a glorious holiday in the Mediterranean, together enjoying the culture and landscape of the beautiful, unspoilt island. And without wishing to boast, despite our – or rather Stephen's – age, our nocturnal endeavours continue to confound medical science and, on occasion, gravity.

All in all, yet another wonderful year I know you'll have delighted in reading about. Merry Christmas and as Happy a New Year as I'm certain we will have.

Much love,
Edna, Stephen and family

PS. Oh, yes, and our baby's doing well. Will send you details of the christening as soon as we've decided on the date, the name and the sex.

Ha! Derivative, unimaginative and aesthetically redundant, my foot! I only hope I didn't go too far. Perhaps I ought to remove the bit about Stephen putting up a shelf . . .

6 Tuesday

Received another email from Mr deClarkson this afternoon. Brangelina's behaviour is still a cause for concern. Apparently, she's been acting the class clown again – and the official class clown isn't happy. I must say, he really has introduced some interesting new initiatives into the school.

7 Wednesday

I'm so proud. Brangelina's got a part in the school nativity. She's the back end of the Virgin Mary. It wasn't quite the role she had been hoping for, it must be said, but as Miss Campbell pointed out, there is no Archangel Herod.

Started to write out my list of presents for the family. Buying for Stephen gets harder every year. I mean, what do you get the man who has . . . well, me? I've scoured my brains. If only they did kebab tokens . . . In the end I gave up and asked him. Not very romantic, I know, but I would never have guessed what he really wanted otherwise – a Thermo-nuclear-octo-robogargantusaur. It's this year's must-have gift, apparently. Honestly, him and his gadgets!

8 Thursday

Bad news. Stephen Junior's musical has been cancelled. The council said it couldn't justify subsidising what had effectively become a one-man show, and the school said it couldn't afford to fund it on the basis of only one family buying tickets. I wonder which family it was?

9 Friday

Stephen's work Christmas do tonight. Of course, being self-employed, it's not a very big occasion. Shame wives aren't allowed.

10 Saturday

Ended up spending all night watching television, waiting for Stephen to get back. Honestly, I don't know what this country's coming to. According to the news, the police have revealed that over 100 major criminals have been traced. They say the police artist has been sacked.

Stephen finally deigned to return at six in the morning. Apparently, this Christmas do was a bit of a disaster. It seems he got way too drunk and told himself what he thought of him before faxing himself a photocopy of his bottom and snogging himself in the supply cupboard. I don't know how he's going to be able to look himself in the eye on Monday morning.

11 Sunday

Stephen's popped out to get the Christmas tree. We've decided to get a real one this year, for once. It's a shame because the kids love the fibre-optic one and it's so much easier to hoover up all those glowing needles, but Stephen hasn't had the chance to use his Debenhams balaclava and chainsaw set yet.

12 Monday

I knew I shouldn't have left Stephen to decorate the house for Christmas! I told him to make it look less like Las Vegas, so he got rid of the giant animatronic Santa. Now there's just Celine Dion and the hookers to go.

13 Tuesday

Bad news. Viennetta failed to get through to the *Now There's a Bit of Talent* Grand Final. She lost out to a sword-swallowing cat with a terminally ill grandmother. I was gutted. That's someone else to cook for on Christmas Day now.

14 Wednesday

Phew! What a day! The Shangri-la centre was packed. At least I managed to get everyone's presents eventually. It was easy enough to get the older kids' gifts (I just bought what they asked for – a 500ml bottle of Chantelle No 5 for Viennetta and Stephen Junior's Hulking Great Brut from More Money Than Scents). I'm sure Brangelina will love her new hamster, complete with cage and wheel of death, and as the twins are completely obsessed with the Telegoths at the moment I've bought them the complete set – Edgar, Alan, Lala and Poe. Then it was straight to the Pawsoleum to get special pet Christmas stockings for Fish, Posh and Tibbles. It might sound a bit silly but we don't indulge them the rest of the year – after all, a pet's for Christmas, not for life.

I did have one uncomfortable moment buying Hugh Junior's magic set when the shop cut up my credit card. Fortunately, when they gave me it back it was in one piece again.

Finally, I bought Stephen's Thermo-nuclear-octo-robogargantusaur. It took hours to track it down as everywhere had sold out. I eventually managed to find one in Toysaurus 'R' Us, and even then I had to fight off three small boys and a lady vicar to get it. I don't really know why I bothered. I can't imagine Stephen doing the same for me. His idea of making an effort is dashing out to the garage before they close on Christmas Eve, and even then it's usually something I don't need, or don't want or doesn't work. In fact, come to think of it, this diary's probably the only thing Stephen's ever bought me that isn't faulty in some way or another.

16 Friday

Spoke too soon.

17 Saturday

Took the twins to Santa's grotto this morning. Well, actually, it was Beardy Pete in the coach station toilets but they seemed to enjoy it. He's really made an effort this year. He had tinsel hanging from the cistern and a cinnamon-scented urinal block. And his lap was far less damp than last Christmas.

18 Sunday

How lovely! It's just started snowing. Isn't nature miraculous? All those beautiful flakes. As I told Subo, although they may appear the same, every single snowflake is completely and totally unique, just like her. Or maybe it was Asbo.

19 Monday

Stephen's having another day off work today – his back's gone again. I warned him not to pick up the Christmas *Radio Times* without warming up properly.

20 Tuesday

The carollers came round again this evening. Still a bit too early, in my book. I told them that they should come back when they've managed to perfect all the harmonies. And that it's still not 'lords a-laying'.

21 Wednesday

Brangelina came shooting home from school today. She couldn't wait to tell us the news. Apparently her classmate, Britnee, had a bit of an accident during the dress rehearsal. Something to do with a runaway truck – I didn't quite catch all the details. Anyway, to cut a long story short, my little girl will be playing the whole of the Virgin Mary tomorrow night! Looks like we've got another thespian in the family!

22 Thursday

We all went along to watch Brangelina in the school nativity this evening. Mr deClarkson greeted all the parents at the entrance to the school hall. It was lovely he'd taken the trouble to remember our names – we were the only parents to have been afforded such an honour, from what I could tell – although I must say his handshake seemed rather less assured than the last time we met and there was a little more saliva on his chin than I remember there being before.

The nativity set was very impressive – Miss Campbell had clearly gone to a great deal of trouble to make it as authentic as possible. Although I have to say I thought all the crucifixes were possibly a touch on the anachronistic side. I didn't mention it to her as she seemed quite fraught as it was. I don't suppose it can be easy organising a performance with excitable little angels like my Brangelina.

It all went very well until the final scene when Miss Campbell tried to hand Brangelina the baby Jesus – played, as ever, by Sharon Reynolds' Little Miss Poopy Pee-pee wrapped in a dog blanket. Instead of taking it and singing 'When a Child Is Born', Brangelina just stared wide-eyed at the little doll. Then all hell broke loose. The windows blew in, thunder cracked and *Carmina Burana* blasted out from the loudspeakers. The audience fled in terror and Miss Campbell cowered behind a children's Bible.

I think, on reflection, Mr deClarkson probably regretted choosing Stephen to man the light and sound system, although we did all enjoy the special effects enormously, once we'd removed the shards of glass from our hair.

Despite the unconventional ending, and rather diminished audience, Mr deClarkson proceeded to give a short speech thanking the children and staff for all their efforts. We were slightly surprised that he chose to give the speech in Swahili and that the bouquet he subsequently presented to Miss Campbell comprised a dozen sticks of rhubarb rather than the more traditional roses, but I suppose it's the thought that counts.

23 Friday

Last day of school before Christmas, so the kids were allowed to take in their toys. So nice to see Mr deClarkson joining in too, even to the extent of having an extremely realistic tantrum and biting one of the Year Three boys when he refused to let him play with his glow-in-the-dark Buzz Lightyear.

Unfortunately, the fun and games were cut short when the school closed early so that police could seal off the area and attempt to talk down a man on the roof with his underpants on the outside of his trousers and his arms aloft, shouting 'Super-head!'

24 Saturday

Christmas Eve. As usual, Stephen's gone out to celebrate but not before insisting the children put out the traditional can of lager and kebab for Santa and his reindeer. He's such a big kid!

'Twas the night before Christmas and right through the town
All the creatures were slurring and tumbling down,
And I, with my nightcap of Horlicks and booze,
Had just settled down for a nice winter's snooze.

When out in the street there arose such a clatter,
That I sprang from my bed to see what was the matter,
And there down below was my very own darling,
Skipping and dancing with eight tins of Carling.

The children awoke thanks to Stephen's daft games
And he sang as he drank and he called out their names:
'Oy Asbo! Oy Subo! Hugh Junior! Viennetta!
Oy Brangie! Oy Junior! I've ruined my sweater!'

His heart and his bladder were filled with good cheer

And several bottles of cheap local beer.
A sudden warm feeling came over him so
He signed us his autograph there in the snow.

He giggled and burped as he reached for his keys,
A difficult task with his pants round his knees,
He took out his dongle – a bit of a worry,
And it shook as he laughed like a bowlful of curry.

Then up on the roof he espied our pet cat,
And he slurred as he shouted, 'What you lookin' at?'
Then he yelled as he slipped and collapsed in a bin,
'Happy Christmas to all, and to all a large gin!'

25 Sunday

Christmas Day! As usual, Stephen was up long before dawn, ripping the paper off his presents. By the time I made it downstairs, he'd been joined by the rest of the kids and they were all merrily playing with their gifts.

Of course, dinner was a triumph. The cranberry-and-lager-glazed roast Spam was as succulent as ever and the sprouts in blankets were done to a turn. My famous sherry trifle, in particular, proved a great success. Just a shame there was no room in the bowl for the cream. Or the custard, sponge or jelly.

The crackers Stephen got from Wee Free Kinks were also a big hit – although, despite clearly winning the pull, I had to let Stephen have the novelty condom with the bell on the tip or I'll never hear the end of it.

After the meal, we all settled round the television to watch this year's special Aardman animation. Naturally, I insisted we all stand up. As I said to the children, plasticine or not, Her

Majesty's still Her Majesty.

After the Queen's Cracking Christmas Message, Stephen and I had our customary Christmas afternoon doze while we left the kids to get the baby down off the top of the tree. Our sleep was interrupted when Viennetta went into labour, but we managed to get off again after a few Quality Streets. Typical that the baby should come today of all days. That's another present I need to get now.

All in all, though, despite everything that's happened recently, I was pleased and relieved that today was just like any other normal Fry Family Christmas Day.

26 Monday

This morning we all went for our traditional Boxing Day family walk. I must say, it was beautiful out there, with the crisp winter sun glinting off the canal. Well, off the shopping trolleys in the canal.

After a lunch of Spam sandwiches, Stephen

finally gave me his Christmas present. Actually, he was several days earlier than usual. And for once it wasn't a car freshener or a bag of charcoal brickettes. In fact, it wasn't from the garage at all – it was a book token for Walter Stone's on the high street. I checked it closely. It looked legitimate enough. I was quite perplexed. Then I spotted it. The small print on the back revealed it was only valid on the 31 December this year. I knew it! He must have got it on the cheap.

Having said that, it's still probably the best Christmas present he's ever given me. And the message in the attached card is terribly sweet:

'To my darling Edna. Merry Christmas. I love you. I thought it was time you knew.'

I have to admit I could feel my eyes welling up, when suddenly from outside I heard the pitch-perfect, word-perfect carollers. They'd clearly taken all my advice to heart and the result was as beautiful as it was uplifting. Such an effort really deserved a huge tip. What a pity they were a day late.

27 Tuesday

Went to the sales this morning. I can't believe how busy it was. I'm amazed I didn't lose one of the kids. It's not as if I wasn't trying.

28 Wednesday

I must say I'm very impressed with the kids' snowman. It's so realistic, slumped against the wheelie bin like that with a half-eaten kebab in its hand. I'm sure even Stephen would be impressed. Talking of whom, I wonder where he's got to? I don't think I've seen him since last night.

29 Thursday

Still no sign of Stephen. Obviously out gallivanting again. I've finally run out of ways to use the turkey. I suppose we may as well eat it now.

30 Friday

So sad to see the snow thaw. The white landscape melt into grey. The magic disappear. On the plus side, I've found Stephen. I'd better get him a jumper.

Once I got Stephen dried off and warmed up, and sent Brangelina and the twins to the naughty step, I sat down to look through the post. Among the bills and junk mail I was surprised to see what looked like a Christmas card. I couldn't imagine the Post Office was to blame – after all, we received all our other cards first thing on the 28th, the same as usual. When I looked closer, I realised the reason for its lateness. It bore a Los Angeles postmark.

Strange, I thought, turning the envelope over and over in my hands. Who on earth did we know in Los Angeles? I was about to tear it open to find out, when it came to me. Of course! That nice, suave, sophisticated, muscular American doctor. Laurie somebody or other, I forget. What was it he said before he left all those months ago? 'It is my sincere hope that we shall meet again'? Or something vaguely like that, I should imagine – I don't really know.

I pursed my lips and carefully pulled open the envelope. I removed the small card with quivering fingers and out fell several sheets of handwritten paper. What did they say? What did he want to tell me? Or ask me?

Unfortunately, I never could read doctors' handwriting.

31 Saturday

Stephen shot out early today without a word. Another window-cleaning emergency, I expect. I hope he gets back in time for tonight's Hogroastmanay Hootenanny at Mrs Norton's.

The kids are all at the mall, and Viennetta's breastfeeding the baby. And her own. I think I'll just have a nice cup of tea and then pop out for a little walk . . .

As I meandered down the street and past the

gasworks my thoughts meandered along with me. A funny day, New Year's Eve. A time of reflection, of fond thoughts and regrets. And a time to look to the future. I wonder what our future will hold? A sudden chill blew through me and I held on to my hat.

Before I knew where I was, I found myself standing cold and alone on the high street. The population of the town must have already made its way to the local hostelries to begin their end of year revelry. No doubt Stephen was with them. I wandered slowly along the pavement, staring blankly at my reflection in the shop windows. I sighed. Who was that woman walking alone down the street in that rather fetching hat? Why was she so sad? What did her life mean? Why was Stephen's face looking back at her?

I blinked. It certainly looked like Stephen. His big, beaming face staring out from that poster.

I took a step back. I looked at the shop sign. Walter Stone's – Purveyor of Fine Literature and Dan Brown Novels. Then at the doorway. Then at the long queue of people that was protruding from it. What was going on?

There was only one way to find out. Steeling myself, I approached the line of people and joined the queue.

After 40 minutes, I finally plucked up the courage to ask the lady in front of me why we were queuing. She looked me up and down with a confused frown.

'It's the book signing, of course!' she said finally. 'Didn't you know?'

'Book signing?' I said. 'What book? Who's signing?'

The woman just laughed and pointed to the poster. 'Who do you think?'

I screwed up my eyes and stared at the poster. It certainly looked like Stephen. But then, how could it be? He was supposed to be on his window-cleaning round. Or in the pub. Or . . .

Oh dear. I felt a cold shudder run through my body. Again. It wasn't the wind this time, though. I looked ahead. The queue was dwindling. Beyond the half-dozen people before me I could make out a table on which was sitting a large pile of books. And next to the pile was . . . someone. I couldn't see his face behind the crowd, just his hand busily scribbling his name.

Could this man . . . this writer . . . this famous writer . . . this famous man . . . be . . . my Stephen? My legs suddenly felt hollow and my stomach began to churn. The queue moved forward.

Suddenly, someone spoke. I looked up. It was a security guard.

'Could everyone please have their money ready to purchase their signed copies?' he asked.

There was a shuffling of paper as people drew out their cash. I automatically reached into my pocket and pulled out my purse. As the queue moved forward again, my shaking hand undid the clasp. I reached inside. Empty! That Brangelina had given herself a pocket money raise! I was about to close my purse and head for the exit when I felt a piece of paper poking out. I unfolded it and held it up. It was the book token. Of course. I checked the date. 31 December – today. What a coincidence! I read the inscription again:

'I love you. *I thought it was time you knew.*'

I swallowed.

The queue edged forward. Now there was only one person between me and the table. Between me and . . . who? What?

'Excuse me, madam.'

I looked up. 'Yes?'

'It's your turn.'

'What?'

'It's your turn now.'

I stared at the guard. Then I noticed something over his shoulder. A flash of red binding and a tantalizing ribbon-marker.

'Excuse me,' I said, pushing past him, brandishing my book token.

So that's that. Another year over. And another to come. Who knows what it will hold?

Whatever it is, at least I've now got my new diary to write it all down in.

But first I think I'll have a nice cup of tea.

Acknowledgements

Oh, hello dears. Are you still here? Well, if you are, here are a few people I'd like to 'thank' for assisting in the publication of my diary and thereby potentially destroying my marriage.

Firstly, Mrs Biggins, Mrs Norton and Mrs Winton, who were all extremely enthusiastic proof-readers, even breaking into my bedside cabinet in order to carry out the task, as I recall.

Secondly, Olivia Guest and Ann Evans of Jonathan Clowes Ltd, who 'persuaded' me that publishing my diary would be – and I quote – 'a good thing.'

And thirdly, the seemingly lovely, 'butter wouldn't melt' Suzie Dooré, now an editorial director at Hodder & Stoughton. And we all know how she got that promotion, don't we, Stephen?

Finally, I would also like to take this opportunity to say a big thank you to all of my lovely, silly Twitter friends. You'll find many of them listed on my Twitter page but here, in hypothetical order, are a few of the loveliest and silliest:

@AlanCBoyle, @ashxyz, @Bluesky107, @caitlinmoran, @CharlotteSykes1, @DaveGorman, @davidschneider, @DawgBelly, @DawnCoxwell, @gavin_bonnar, @izzywizzy80, @jonholmes1, @justVero, @karencleary, @laurashav, @MorganRitchie, @ourmissingcat, @Raymondstar, @RedDandy, @RussBass, @Sharon_Corr, @toniwilliamsz, @TweetingTimesEd, @veraclaythorne and @wendyfarrowart.

Well, thank goodness that's all over. Now, where's that teapot?